International Generalizations

-what's the point of this page? I'm just going to have to print it again with the subtitle...

'*International Generalizations*'
Written by Carl Brodersen
Some parts glanced at editorially by Señor Srekcleov (gracias!)

Published by CHCB
   Juneau, Alaska, 99801
Via Lulu.com
   http://www.lulu.com/

Copyright © 2007 by Carl Brodersen, all rights reserved.
Go ahead and use stuff for fun or education though (hopefully it's both).
But if you make anything off of using this, be sure to cut me in.

ISBN 978-0-6151-5678-1 <- !!!!

(Did you see that? I got an ISBN! sa-*weet*!)

'*International Generalizations: Swanky Color Version*' also available

International Generalizations
A "charming" account of a college Junior's European Journey

-see?

-Forward-
[On the off chance that someone who isn't related to me actually reads this]

Howdy-do! My name is Carl. I live in Juneau, Alaska, am 5' 10", enjoy holding hands during long walks on the beach, and am only mildly narcissistic.

In the Spring of 2006, I decided to see whether all the French teachers I'd had since high school were just making things up or not and arranged to go on your standard junior-year-of-college-study-abroad-adventure. I left the familiar, wheat-intensive surrounds of Whitman College in Walla Walla, Washington, and headed off for a semester at the Burgundy School of Business (*École Supérieure de Commerce de Dijon*) in Dijon, France (if you think of France as being like Washington, Dijon would be the Spokane).

During this time I learned that travel is all about the *differences* you find. Sure, the good food and attractive locals are a major part of the experience, but the best reason to go is to learn about the things we'd never be able to know if we stayed at home. The most popular national oddities we can pick up on through the course of normal living -and indeed, before making the trip this basic knowledge can be critical *("hey wait a minute, these people are all talking in French!?")*- but the most thrilling differences are all the *little things* -the ones unavailable to us since they are rarely transmitted back through the typical channels of information because of their apparent inconsequentiality [for example, did you know that one of the literal translations of the French term for *love handles* (*poignées d'amour*) is 'love doorknobs'?]. The only means of hearing about these gems is to have a friend with an enormously undemanding social life go abroad and take the time to write home about them, and since this is clearly done at the expense of other activities, you feel morally obligated to read it all, though my goodness it goes on....

    France provided a limitless supply of *little things*, and I felt it was my civic duty to alert the folks back home to my exciting discoveries ["their light bulbs are different!"]. This book is a compellation of the mass e-mails I sent to friends and family during my trip. I've tried to stay as true to the original material as possible- refraining from adding fiction, and keeping things like the eclectic title and paragraph formatting (which is *way* easier than making it all consistent). If anything in this text strikes you as a bit odd (like the subject lines that have nothing to do with the content that follows, or the excessive hyphenation and creative use of commas), assume that I did it on purpose to make you think. This also applies to typos, formatting errors, misspellings, flagrant inaccuracies, and anything that seems slanderous. Absolutely nothing in these pages is real, even the true parts. Please don't sue me for libel.

    Finally, I'd like to say Thank You to the original letter recipients who encouraged me to inflict them on others. Their confidence, along with the image I conjured up of me handing my grandparents a book with my name on it, have led to this: *International Generalizations*; 175 pages of broad conclusions collectively applied to entire nations based on really small sample sizes, and all in the passive voice. Golly it's good stuff. Enjoy!

    -Carl

Pour Madame

-Introduction-

They, the *Already Traveled*, bubbling over with endless tales of their own wondrous journeys, will never neglect to tell us about all the pitfalls we'll be facing during our impending travels. They'll speak of the homesickness and how it can be unbearable (watch out for that big lull after the first high in the second month). They will fill us full of trepidation describing horrible experiences with thieves and scoundrels, against whom we should be ever vigilant. And then there's always that huge list of things to never ever do there (that somehow you've never heard any of) because in the country where you're going, that innocuous little action is actually some kind of unforgivable insult, might land you in jail, is an unbreakable commitment to wed this skeezy creep who's been hitting on you all night, is an *actual* and *legally binding* vow of marriage, or is just some horribly awkward social faux pas that will mark you and anyone who looks like you in that town for the rest of the century. You shouldn't worry though, in truth; the worst part of it all is the paperwork before you even get on the plane.

Getting a French visa is a struggle, despite Schengen. After filling out all the proper forms and gathering the necessary documents, U.S. residents of the west coast must go in person to either the consulate in San Francisco or (at least when I did it) the sub-office in Seattle. This is a pain, but only fair since the U.S. is being less than cordial these days about our own entry requirements.

I went to the Seattle office where I waited in the lobby with my application worrying that I had missed some requirement, was eventually called in to do even more paperwork, then had my picture taken ("Non, vraiment, I think eet looks great") and, finally, was fingerprinted for the first time ever -information which was no doubt shared with our own government as a 'courtesy'. It was a long wait, and the fingerprinting puts me at a significant disadvantage when it comes to a possible future as a bank robber. But, on the upside, the scanner that does it was super cool and had this neat no-glare screen and lots of flashy lights. And during the whole event I had the opportunity to join the French staffers in some friendly Belgium-bashing (Belgium, being smaller than France, rents a single room in the French office for their one resident diplomat. This poor person is ripped on endlessly, though in a very good-natured way where you get the feeling that the French quietly admire him).

     A few weeks after the results of that meeting are mailed off to the main consulate, San Francisco will get in touch with you regarding the parts of your application that were left out even though the good folks in Seattle didn't mention anything about them at all, and a few weeks after that they'll finally send you back your passport with a shiny new sticker in it featuring a really bad photo of you.

     And then, really, you're all set. Someone might still make you worry about forgetting how to speak English once you've come back, saying that they knew someone who could only babble in incoherent Franglais pidgin for a whole month afterwards, or that you'll never readjust to your old school after being abroad and you'll have to drop out, or worry you that the reverse culture shock will be so strong when you get back that you'll want to renounce your citizenship and move to Canada to be a hermit [If no one has in fact done any of this for you yet you really should have skipped most of this section] – Anyway to all this I say Bah! Just remember: once you have all the paperwork done, that's the last big obligation you'll have (I mean, besides any classes you might be taking), and though realistically speaking, the French will probably try to stick you with some more paperwork while you're there just for good measure[1], the rest should be a breeze.

At least in theory :)

(Oh and don't drink the water.)

---

[1] Since it's in another zip code you can probably ignore it with no repercussions. Or they might deport you. Hey, it's an adventure.

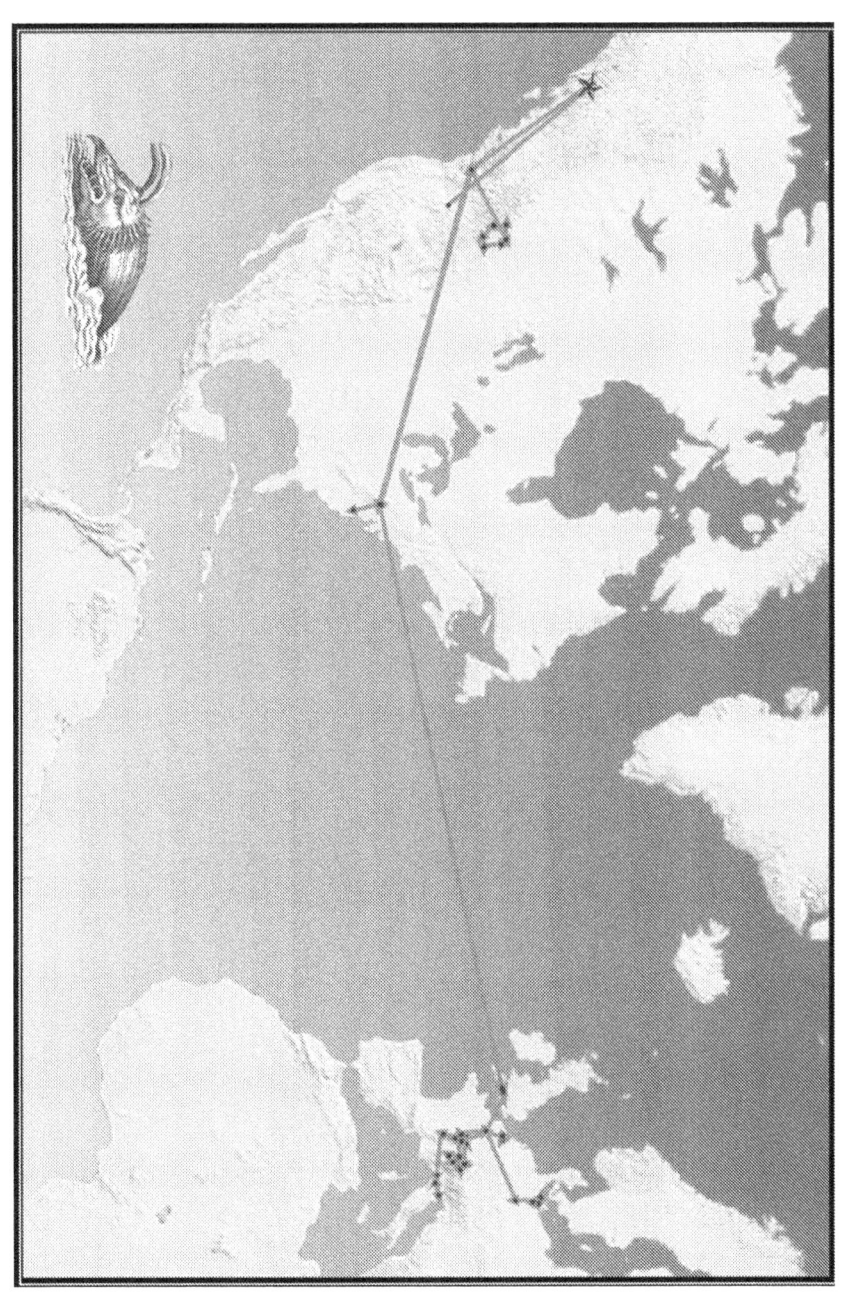

-The known world-

International Generalizations
C. Harold Brodersen

-and here it is *again* ! On the the final go-around you include the title image once more
(it's an entire nation in a box- kind of a metaphor for the book).
(Trust me it's brilliant).

Subject: **My pre-France first mass e-mail (no Internet as of yet, but that won't affect you until you get this)**
Date: **Sunday, 15 Jan 2006, 07:04**

-I'm at gate 17 of Heathrow airport, awaiting the flight to Paris. Bloody marvelous!

When I came through English customs I had the opportunity to observe *in action* one of the peaks of upper-class travel in Britain: access to the FastTrack® program, which, for what I'm sure is only a modestly outrageous sum, gets you through check-in and security more quickly via a special VIP line that lets you bypass all the peasants. I think there's complementary tea involved somehow too. Since my money isn't worth diddly over here I opted out, but I'll take a lesson from it; in the name of brevity I'll make you all upper-class readers of this as well as any future e-mails and provide free access to a fast track for your convenience...

Fast track:

Made it as far as London.
London is not like America.
British accents kick ass.
All is well.

Peasant track:

I'm still impressed by the fact that all of this is actually here; the airport, England, Europe –it's great, this means my teachers and history books and the Internet weren't all colluding to engineer a giant false reality to serve as a cover for their diabolical mind experiments. This is good.

The feeling of amazement started as soon as I could see it all out the jet's window, in the mists of early morn'. It's an almost mythical place, one out of legend and fairy tales, but by golly, there it was below, people driving on the wrong side of the road and everything. Magic.

Earlier during what I'm going to call "today" I got to visit part of the Smithsonian with some friends from Juneau who were nice enough to drive two hours from their home in West Virginia to save me from a twelve-hour layover at Dulles. It was a delight. We looked at the museum for a while and then I fell asleep in their car.

Before D.C. I spent a few days in Seattle doing last minute shopping with my father [hi Dad!], as well as visiting other wonderful friends who all wanted to say goodbye before the big trip incase the plane crashed or I end up saying the wrong thing about cheese to someone. It was a lovely send-off, thank you all.

The aircraft for the Atlantic crossing was a 777, which was a new experience for me. I'm used to smaller planes. As such I almost laughed out loud back at the terminal in D.C. when I turned a blind corner in the jetway and found it was ramped up to a 20° angle to get up to the plane's hatch.

The engines on a 777 are very quiet, but only once they reach a sufficient rate of rotation. Until then they're painful to be near and sound like cybernetic whales bellowing at one another while you're trying to get some shuteye.

From Seattle to D.C. I was on a 737-700 –the 700 part also being a new aviation experience for me. Both jets featured incredibly flexible wings that probably cut down on shaking from air turbulence, but the way they wobbled sure made it look like they were going to snap off if too many air molecules hit them at the wrong angle.

The gates here at Heathrow are denoted with fabulous blue neon signs. Most of the ceilings are absolutely no taller than they need to be, except on the main concourse, creating a neat cave-like effect that's enhanced by the use of plastic grills for the ceilings instead of the soundboard most of us are used to, and also by the excellent use of angled granite flashing at the base of the walls. Still, I can't give this place more than a seven; it's outgrown itself, and the security screening they ran us through had only three stations, one of which had a broken metal detector, while the third was for those upper-class Fast Track passengers only (which is fine so long as it never stands empty while there is a line for the other two, which it did).

The racial diversity is much more comprehensive than I'm used to, and seems to span the different class lines nicely.

The symbol for the ladies' room looks like she's wearing a hooped skirt. It's cute. I wouldn't want to go to the bathroom wearing one of those though.

There are real French people sitting next to me! Almost in their natural habitat! Oh gosh this is exciting, I feel like David Attenborough. It's scary too though, I have no idea what they're saying to each other and somehow I need to be able to communicate well enough to find the appropriate bus and train once I get to Paris.

Okay, I have a few minutes still and I've been flying for a day straight, I'm going to head off and try to take a sponge bath in the gents' room.
Cheerio!
     -Carl

Subject: First France mass e-mail (first Internet access)
Date: Tuesday, 17 Jan 2006, 12:10

Fast track:

Hi! I'm in France. If you didn't know I was planning this we should really hang out more often, my bad.
Made it to Dijon.
Reminds me of Disneyland.
It's raining.

Peasantrack:

I arrived in Dijon later than planned, but intact. The hardest part -the transfer from Paris's CDG airport to the Gare de Lyon train station- went just fine (I was aided in my endeavor by a ski bum from Malaysia who was also coming from the airport, and a nice Parisian gentleman who pointed us towards the right metro stop after seeing us grimacing in front of a route map for ten minutes, lost, wondering how long we could survive on the tufts of grass growing under the sign). On the way I think I even caught a glimpse of the Eiffel Tower, but it was so brief I can't be sure (the shuttle bus was going about mach 2).

    Once I arrived at the station, though, I had trouble finding my train south. I had made it to the platform in plenty of time so I just waited next to the main information board for details on from which lane my train would depart. The lanes are clearly labeled A through N. When mine finally popped up, it said it was departing from #17. Difficulty ensued.

Anyway, an hour and one non-refundable ticket later I finally made it. I was greeted at the station by students from the school's international program, and it turned out the guy up the aisle a few seats from me who looked like he would fit in perfectly in Boston was, in fact, from Boston, and heading to the same program as me. Our friendly greeters put all our bags (I had fewer than Boston, and thus win at life) in the back of a Renault and drove us into the depths of the city center. I actually have a pretty good sense of direction, but I was utterly lost after about thirty seconds.

There are going to be twenty of us in the American program at the école this semester. We're being put up in a hotel for a few days as we wait for everyone to arrive, and to get used to the place during a time of no scholastic obligations while the staff can watch us like hawks. Once we've acclimated a bit we'll meet our host families, and then start classes at the ESCD in about two weeks. As is often the case with French-related programs, the "ratio" is pretty good... I won't spell it out blatantly, but I will say that there are three of us staying in Chambre 221, and it's the only guys' room (misogynistic high-fives all around).

Dijon feels old to the point that it's almost laughable, as opposed to the U.S. east coast, which is just un-humorously "vintage". This place is an architectural nightmare of old and new, though I think they prefer to use the word 'quaint.' I have a sneaking suspicion that the look is going to grow on me a lot. I think another term for *nightmare* is *treasure trove*.

To my surprise, Dijon has a mini Arc de Triumph, which apparently is actually very common in French cities -the one in Paris just happens to be the one in Paris (and huge).

After seeing an evening here, I've decided that the secret to a lively city nightlife is having no sidewalks- since it means the streets are all one big unit that can be crossed freely. That way they're not at divisive as they would be otherwise. And the pedestrian-only areas put everything on a human level and it's a lot easier for a person to spend money than a car. It also makes it easier for revelers to become 'chemically enhanced' without getting hit by moving vehicles.

The ancient city streets that now carry high levels of traffic have been paved-over in some areas. It's nice for cars, but when they repave, they just add more asphalt to what's already there without grinding off any of the old layers. Eventually the streets will be higher than the sidewalks (they do have sidewalks here, but they're fair game for cars, so watch out).

A guy at a restaurant asked if I was Kevin Costner. I'm still not sure why, but found it highly amusing. I was eating with six girls, but Costner's not that big a ladies' man I'd bet (nor am I, for the record, at least not yet anyway), so I remain mystified.

This e-mail as well as the previous one that accompanies it was brought to you by CABAUT, who seems to live near the hotel lobby and doesn't have a password on his wireless hub. Myself and the twelve other net-addicted Americans sitting here by the front door are eternally grateful.

    -Carl

Subject: **More France!**
Date: **Sunday, 22 Jan 2006, 13:26**

Fast track:

Host family seems okay, young children cute. Will be fairly independent on the whole, but that has its pluses.
Went on class tour to nearby wine country and historical sights (Hôtel Dieu).
Still not a fan of wine but the history part was cool.
Have taken first pictures of ancient European cathedral, am now officially a tourist.
Cooked the first of my meals - results non-lethal, will probably survive rest of trip.
This Russian dude on TV is a pretty good skater (the Olympics, like math, are fun in all languages).

Othertrack:

Life: The family I live with is nice. The house is getting on near three-hundred years old (allergies might be a problem, we'll see). It of course has the R-value from hell, and like most French they keep the heat lower than we do, so I'm enjoying typing because of the radiation from my computer.

The family has two apartments. The main one is on the second story, but I'm downstairs at street-level, where the noise is intense (I might need to become a heavier sleeper). The Street really is a bigger part of life here, whether you like it or not.

There are four kids: two older ones who live nearby, and then there are the very cute Jean-Paul and François who are 8 and 10 maybe? I should ask. Since I thought from the dossier the study abroad people sent me that all the kids were young and still living here, these two made out like bandits on the age-oriented welcome gifts I brought.

The parents are semi-divorced, as far as I can tell. Everyone shares living space, but the dad has his room downstairs, and the mom has yet to appear on the ground floor. They seem to be very amiable with each other; helping each other out, eating dinner as a family- but that might just be for the benefit of the kids, I can't tell. On the upside, it means I only have a guy to judge my tidiness. Also a plus is that he has studied other languages so he understands the situation we're in (people who never have seem to lack the right sort of patience).

I get the feeling that I'm more of a boarder than a temporary family member who will have a framed portrait on the mantle for years to come (I'm their tenth student; some families here are on their 30th). That works though. I only have to worry about periodic family dinners (which have been a hoot so far -excellent cheese selection), and having that downstairs kitchen pretty much all to myself the rest of the time is going to be great, so it's all good.

My room is what I'd call typical size and has a nice simplicity to it. There's even an old power converter that one of their previous students left. It's enormous though, about three times the size of the one I brought and heavy (I'm surprised it's not made of cast iron) so I think I'll stick with mine. There's a computer upstairs with dial-up, and, for some utterly incomprehensible reason, AOL. Why go out of your way to use American crap when there's plenty of your own available? I hope the computers at school are more amenable.

The kids have the typical computer games about warring medieval empires to play on –knights and castles and all that. I wonder if the games feel any different when the empires in question of the precursors of your own nation.

Also, they apparently they make a French version of Grand Theft Auto.

School: Classes start next week, so I can continue to avoid thinking about them.

Travel!: They organized a bus trip for us to the nearby countryside. We saw some sites, including the nearby (everything's nearby when your from Alaska) and very old

Hôtel Dieu has a nice roof (Burgundy is famous for colorful and elaborate glazed tile roofs), and is a good example of trying to buy your way into Heaven after a life of misdeeds (the builder felt bad for embezzling cash from the local Duke, so he used the money to build a hospital and named after God. Smooth move). During the tour we learned that there exists such as thing as the *mustard enema,* which was more popular than leeches at the time (those two together being the only non-invasive medical options available for a couple hundred years).

Afterwards, we had a private tour of the family winery of one of our program directors. The ceilings of the cellars were COVERED with dark brown mold. Allergy-wise, I'm surprised I survived. The wine was good, but I still haven't been converted to the bacterial excrement in liquid form camp, I only like it in semi-solid gel mode. It was a neat operation to look at though.

There is a lot of interesting history in the French wine industry. Apparently in the late 1800s there was an epidemic of a root louse called phylloxera that destroyed something like two thirds of the vines (which take years to grow) in Europe. The solution, much to the chagrin of the purist French vintners, was to graft French vines onto louse-resistant North American rootstalks (oh the indignity!). In so doing, they were able to combat the phylloxera but without being forced to switch to American grapes, some of which were felt to have notes of a malodorous after-taste that the professionals call "fox piss." America saves the day! [Of course, bearing in mind the biological implications of this natural resistance, we won't mention where the phylloxera probably came from in the first place.]

For the Engineers: We visited some really interesting sites, including a 400-odd year-old roofed marketplace. The roof was made entirely of stone (we're talking rocks here, not cut slabs) held up by wood timbers. The joints were mostly mortice and tenon held by thin little pins, all completely desiccated and shriveled. It's hard to have building codes and standardization when stuff lasts so long.

Observations: As one would expect, history rules here. Rather than rebuild, interiors are endlessly modernized while exteriors are left in original condition, and structural integrity is maintained through any means necessary to keep old buildings from falling apart (think huge metal bars with blocks at each end stuck through a house from one side to the other too keep the walls from blowing out. It's all about the houses here, not so much the people who live in them it seems. History is important, sure, but so is progress. Maybe what we think is progress is just change.

The spiraling stairs in 'E' building of the ESCD are backwards -meaning that if people with swords were attacking and defending, those advancing from the bottom (the invaders) would have an advantage as the majority of them would be right-handed and able to use the central pillar for cover, while the defenders above would be forced to expose themselves to fight back. This worries me greatly because 'E' building houses the support staff for all the foreign students, without whom we'd be completely and utterly lost- and you never know when Vikings are going to show up.

Considering the amount of dog feces on the sidewalks the nationwide shoes-OK-inside policy is surprising.

On TV they like to put computer-animated characters in places where they're glaringly out of place ('Why's this guy animated? -they clearly just green-screened an actor in a suit, why not use the original?'). French popular TV ranks right down there with the Mexican Soap Opera.

French TV ads like to tantalize viewers with certain parts of a certain gender's bodies to a degree that would scandalize even the raciest of Superbowls. Yay for cultural differences :)

                -Carl

Subject: **Ahoy**
Date: **Thursday, 26 Jan 2006 17:38**

Fast track:

S'all good.

Other track:

The school has a huge contingent of international students, maybe even as many as a hundred, and I think we have people from every continent (I'm just sure I saw a penguin the other day). There're some pretty cool folks here. Sadly, it's turning out there isn't exactly an over-abundance of coolness amongst the Americans here -yours truly excepted of course (this has been confirmed by several Frenchies and at least one German, and the Greek guy didn't say anything but I could tell he was thinking it). In all fairness, I'm sure my expatriate compatriots would say the same about me, but there's one important consideration on that point; they don't have your e-mail address. There are a few gems of course -every pile of dirt has a few- but having finally had a chance to spend time in groups composed of people from multiple countries all interacting as citizens of a world -with a few stupid Americans present for contrast- I've come to see how much we live up to our reputation for being ignorant, loud, boorish, self-centered –in general: *totally lame*. (I'm glad none of you are like that :)

    It's been fairly easy to make friends so far. The non-American exchange students are really good at being open and meeting folks, so all it takes is an in with one or two of them and you've got a huge group of great people to hang out with and learn from (and like I said, some of the American students are more than okay too).

    Yesterday I went to a laser tag game with a bunch of locals and other exchange students, as organized by the schools international club, Melting Potes (*potes* being French for chums/friends -how clever!). It was a real hoot. My game stats were middle-of-the-road (all guys like to

think they can be 007 Rambo John Wayne types with no training beyond having watched *'3 Ninjas'* when it came out in the fourth grade), but it was a good time nonetheless. Had a wild ride in a French car on the way home and met two neat guys from Finland.
-By the way, here they call it "laser game", in English.

It snowed today, about an inch and a half of soft/wet. It was a nice surprise.

I think my address here is:
   Carl Brodersen - Programme U.S.
   ESCDijon
   29 rue Sambin
   21000 Dijon
   FRANCE

Some brave soul should send a postcard so we can see if it works before any of you risk sending a box of gold bars, we wouldn't that getting lost in the mail.

Since starting to cook for myself this week I have still yet to drop dead, so chances are good that I'll be able to survive the semester. Adjust your wagers accordingly.

My host père is a big WWII fan, so I've seen a few documentaries since arriving. The stock footage the French use in their productions is quite different. It focuses much more on the human aspect of war, and includes lengthy personal interviews recorded at the time or just after –something I don't recall ever seeing back home.
        Also on that front, it appears that Host Père is seeing someone - she comes over on weekends. The whole arrangement is a bit unorthodox, but imagine how much better-off the kids are having both parents around.

In France "hors d'oeuvres" is singular, and actually refers to the main course. Somehow we screwed that one up.

Cheerio!
        -Carl

Subject: **France Attacks!**
Date: **Sunday, 28 Jan 2006, 19:25**

Slowly everyone gets added to the list, apologies to those who have had to wait, I blame this crazy French computer and Microsoft for making it impossible (so far) to use my Apple laptop on the school's system [I mean *honestly, who* makes their PPP client server use MS-CHAP v2 with 64-bit encryption as the front for their VPN *in a school? I mean come one people!*].

Fast track:

I am a phenomenal nerd.
Shopping sucks here too-

Other track:

-at least on weekends. I took a bus to the local huge disgusting mall complex, the Toison D'Or. This means "*Golden Fleece*" so naturally I checked to see if the bus was named the *Argo*. It wasn't. It was the *#23*. I think they missed an opportunity on that one.

Anyway, my mission was to hit up a Fred Meyers-esque chain store called Carrefour ("*Crossroads*"). I'm sure the stuff at in the neighborhood markets is better, but I wanted to see how a superstore would look in a country that is rewound for despising them. It was a zoo. Next time I'll try a weekday afternoon, on a cold day, maybe during Lent, when it's closed... yeah that aughta do it.

Readily available at Carrefour ("*Crossroads*") were a few standout items, including quail eggs by the dozen, whole rabbit, and big empty snail shells for escargot-related fare.

All the prices are indicated by tiny LCD screens (like those on a clock). I bet that investment pays for itself in about a year (provided batteries last long enough).

Perhaps the greatest discovery was that kielbasa is readily

available in <u>2-inch diameter</u> units – there's none of this piddly 1.25-inch silliness we have in the states. I can only imagine what Germany would be like.

Sausage in general is available in countless shapes and varieties- all of which I must sample of course (meaning that the chances behind something I've eaten recently resembling another certain something that a dog left behind on the sidewalk recently will be pretty bad).

The first pomelos I encountered here was smaller than a grapefruit, much to my alarm, but specimens of the ridiculous size I'm used to at home were available at Carrefour, much to my delight. They come in three scrumptious varieties: "*plain*", "*white*", and "*from China*".

I've been informed by a real French person that *hors d'oeuvres* (which I totally just spelled right on the first try go me) *are*, in fact, little snacky things that often come on toothpicks before a meal, just as we all thought before I reported otherwise. I guess we can all rest assured that we're not crazy, and of course won't think one little bit about the accuracy of anything else I've written.

Navigating the town is slowly getting easier. I'm surprised by how often I find myself wandering in some direction, utterly lost, and then five meters later suddenly discover that I'm at a large landmark and am actually quite close to where I wanted to be. And the route home is easy to find now, just follow the movie posters: it's a left at '*Munich*', straight past '*Les Invitées*', and then a right at '*Bambi II*'. I'll be lost again as soon as they change the posters though. Darn film industry.

Was denied entry to a disco for wearing sweatpants (bright white, no stains -quite dashing I felt). The bouncer said I couldn't come in looking like I was out jogging. Fortunately I was too tired to make a fuss at the time, but now I'm miffed by how pretentious that was (a proper jacket for a 5-star I can understand, but the right pants for a disco?). Someday

I'll have to go back properly dressed, gain entry, and then change into something hideous in the bathroom.

The pharmacies here all have signs made of large equilateral crosses comprised of dancing green neon tubes -conceptually reminiscent of the U.S. barber shop sign, but far more Swiss-Irish in practice.

Far too much smoking is going on.

Rearranged the furniture in my room to make it more practical and usable. It also feels a little more like it's mine now. It's nice to be able to put one's own stamp on things.

-__/§-*Carl*-§__-

Subject: **France objects!**
Date: **Thursday, 2 Feb 2006, 16:34**

Fast track:

Went to a wine festival.
The gym at the school is run by fascists.
Experienced my first French labor strike (they're famous for them).
...oh yeah; classes!

Bored right now = makes reading these easier track:

Wine Festival: Last weekend I went to a festival that covered a big chunk of the region (the '*wine region of France*,' to be specific). The annual festival is held to honor St. Vincent, the patron saint of wine (who by the way they're pretty sure never touched the stuff). There were about forty small villages that all house vineyards and wine cellars, divided into four bus routes with service about every twenty minutes, and hundreds of people riding between them in various states of shall we say 'giddiness.' They were all decorated according to a seasonal theme (the villages I mean, not the giddy people... well, some people were by the end actually), and all the wine cellars were open for tasting and business.

For the participation fee, every participant was given a tiny silver cup called a *tastevin* for partaking of the available wine samples. Essentially a shallow saucer with a teacup handle, the device was actually invented here in Burgundy by its expert wine makers and sommeliers. They're convex on the bottom and multi-faceted to reflect as much light as possible, the colors of the silver and the various dimensions having been painstakingly calculated after years of research and product refinement to maximize the tastevin's efficiency and functionality for the purpose of assessing the colors of wines stored in dark, candle-lit sellers. By the way the French Economy is in the toilet right now. Just thought I'd mention.

The truly hardcore participants, in contrast, brought their own *long-stem crystal* wine glasses, that they hung around their necks on neon orange neoprene lanyards for easy access. These people were amazing.

The whole event was a great opportunity to see *lots* of the surrounding region once I realized that it was more fun to just stay on the buses and look at the scenery -rather than get off at each stop to admire the towns up close, so I just bus-hopped and eventually settled on one with a humorous driver. In a country like France, that's not the most outgoing of them all, it was nice to find a resident who was gregarious and extraverted. I'm pretty sure he was Italian.

The bus drivers here are superheroes. All the coaches are seven gears forward manual, and, despite the very close wheel placement specially designed for the tiny roads, seem to only clear the priceless antique buildings by about an inch at every corner. The Italian guy was very talented; he could take corners that the bus in front of us had to approach, stop, reverse turn, and go at again ("Quelle disgrace!"). We made a point of cheering for him every time he made a maneuver the bus in front of us couldn't.

I've recently discovered that *7up* and red wine go together really well at around a 50:1 ratio. Of course, I had no *7up* with me during the festival, so I paid due homage to St. Vincent by doing as he did(n't). A great time was had, and my tastevin isn't all sticky so I can hang it on the wall as a memento. I feel a bit guilty coming to one of the greatest wine-producing areas of France not liking to imbibe much, but Franco-U.S. relations have survived worse.

Gym: There's a large room here intended to be a gym that I found bereft of life yesterday, occupied only by dusty, second-hand equipment shoved into a corner, and a pile of dirty exercise mats. The place didn't appear to have been used in years, so I spent two hours moving a couple hundred pounds of machines, weights, and benches into what I deemed to be their proper positions; with much consideration given to safety, clearance, type of exercise, flow of human traffic, direction of attention/gaze, and overall sustainability of the layout. I even organized the dirty mats by color. The place was <u>gorgeous</u> when I left.

It turns out this morning that there's an aerobics club that meets there once a week, at most, and they had moved everything back aside into random piles. It struck me as akin to a farmer shoving an expensive tractor out of a barn and into the rain to make room for a hand plow. To each their own I guess.

Labor: I saw my first government worker strike today! The French are famous for these, so boy was I excited. [Their frequency is one of the things we foreigners learn about when our French language classes cover culture - that, and the incredible quantity of dog doo on the sidewalks.] They were upset about education funding and/or teacher salaries. [See photo.]

Classes: are three hours long and once a week. I'm usually done at 7:00 in the evening. So far quality has varied but all will be interesting in one way or another by virtue of their being in French. Mostly I have politics-esque and business-ish-related courses. Sadly, it turns out German and Russian both conflict with morning classes I'm obliged to take, so no additional language classes for me here.

En general: Many of the power lines are supported by concrete poles instead of metal or wood. I've come to really miss wood. Most of the construction here is done with limestone since it's so abundant (that's also the reason the rivers are all yellow -though I like my pure-liquid-jaundice theory a whole lot more). I don't think wood has the same degree of acceptance as a building material that it does back home. Back in high school a German exchange student friend of mine was amazed when I told him his host family was actually quite wealthy –"But their house is made of wood!"

I don't care what cultural anthropologists say about judging others' customs, the people here are not safe drivers, it just happens that everyone is at the same level of recklessness so it creates the impression of order. I think part of it is that the concept of *proximity* is different. The personal bubble between people is smaller, and that notion extends to cars as well, making the acceptable range for passing a pedestrian at 90 kmh about half a meter. And turn signal use seems to be illegal, based on the frequency at which it occurs.

Well it's late, and I haven't eaten yet -time to go be a gourmand.
-by which I do mean go melt cheese onto something.
    -Carl

grève.jpg

Subject: **More broad generalizations!**
Date: **Monday, 6 Feb 2006, 12:26**

Fast track:

Another grocery experience -slightly less craziness.
Classes continue to be... interesting.
Resistance was futile - I bought a temporary cell phone.
-06.77.64.80.20
-Feel free to call me at 4AM.
-Your time that is, that's the middle of the afternoon over here.
-Don't call me at 4AM my time.
-Unless you really want to.
-Or if you're my friend Karl, in which case it's just desserts (apologies again).

Howdy-do!:

Shopping:
Every time I look at a receipt for something I've bought I first see the for-comparison-purposes price listed in French Francs, printed under the real one in Euros, and freak out: "What!?? wha!!?-two hundred thirty-seven Eur-oh, okay, oh man thank goodness...."

The Carrefour staff move around on rollerblades because the store is so large. This is great news. Now if my plan to be a bike cop at SeaTac airport doesn't pan out I have another dream job to fall back on.

Produce is weighed not at the checkout stands, but at a special station where it is given a bar code that the checkout stand reads later. At the same time, bags are sealed by a handy little tape machine; it cuts off a length of tape, twists up the bag, and sticks it on all in one smooth motion (I just realized while typing this that this is done to prevent the addition of more produce after applying the barcode: *Checker-outer:* "Monsieur, the label on this bag says it has one apple in it, and yet it contains six canta-loupes and a whole duck. Can you explain?" This is a sad realization because I thought the taping was for our convenience. Now I'm all disillusioned).

All the shopping carts at the Toison D'Or are managed by the mall itself, not just the Carrefour. You can take them anywhere in the whole building, and there are stair-less escalator ramps set at about 20° to accommodate them.

General:
All the crutches here are of the sort that has a cup for your upper arm to rest in and a handle set perpendicular to the main upright. I've seen this style used in the US by folks who will need them long-term, but we're still issuing the 'standard' ones for shorter duration uses. The European-style ones are much better for your underarms, and I think are cheaper too. Darned habits.

At the train station last weekend, on my way to the wine festival, there was a sign saying that due to inclement weather they were limiting the trains to 230*km/h* and that the inconvenience was regretted. "<u>limiting</u>." Wow. *Va-voom*.

The electrical outlets here are built large, to match the large round plugs that go into them, so anything plug-related is accordingly huge. I saw an octopus (the eight plug electrical accessory kind, not the cephalopod) with the usual on/off breaker on one end that was well over two feet long! The sockets are deeply recessed too, necessitating that the plugs be larger in that direction so the octopus was about an inch and a half thick! It's all quite cumbersome. Minus 5!

They get points back for the grounding pins though, unlike the ones from home, they're part of the socket, not the plug. The plug has either a corresponding socket or, if it doesn't need a ground, just a gap to accommodate the pin. This is much handier than the other way around that we have, which frequently results in people cutting off their grounding pins when things don't fit, which is dangerous.

International Generalizations

There is way too much camera work going on in French television. Back and forth, split screen, pan up, pan down - it's ridiculous. One show will even do overhead shots of the camera we were just looking through for a second instead of switching straight to showing the new angle and what's actually going on. And they never leave the camera still either, they're always cutting from one to another. On a music awards show the other night the average shot duration was just *four* seconds, with the overall record only *eight* seconds! I think this is another form of the flashy graphics they use in the US to bombard you with so much imagery that your brain can't process it all at once –which makes you impulsively look at it more intently trying to comprehend it all. Boy that's annoying. One thing that does *not* appear to be happening here though is ads having higher volume levels compared to the shows. Good for them on that one.

A lot of the shows are from nearby countries and dubbed into French. One out of Germany features a helicopter rescue team in Berlin that goes around saving people and avoiding character development. The plots aren't that complicated, nor are the emergencies all that gripping. Really, I think the only reason they even include the people in need is so that they have a legitimate excuse for the helicopter to take off three or four times per episode of full of solemn-looking young crew members in military gear with dramatic electric guitar riffs playing. That's not much of a basis for a show, but clearly you can get by on less.

Cut an onion in half and then freeze it. It looks awesome. Cooks differently too.

School:
The class structure here is odd ("different"). All but one of mine are three hours long with one break in the middle, once a week, starting at 9:45 or 14:00. My language class is three times a week in the evenings, 17:30 - 19:00. Nada on Fridays but I might fill that with an internship if the

school's *stage* organizer ever finds something appropriate (my résumé looked pretty funny translated -and truncated- into French).

Most of the classes seem to be 'thought exercises' as opposed to the 'learning of specific things to be applied later,' at least I think so (might just be a difference in perspective). The French are supposed to be very theory and process-oriented so I guess this makes sense, but I bet I'll develop a stronger appreciation for the classes back at Whitman - as well as an appreciation for the methods of ESCDijon once I'm back in Walla Walla. Grass is always greener...

Class descriptions:
I have an e-commerce class that involves lots of group work and a professor for whom French and English are both second languages (he speaks Persian). He keeps jumping between his two second languages mid-sentence. It actually works amazingly well. 'Culture and French society' is a hoot, I like the prof. a lot (turns out it's the fellow who took us to his winery) and the organization of the material is wonderfully familiar -probably a reflection of the amount of time he's spent observing Anglo-Saxon culture in action (his wife is English). 'Key economic and Social issues in Western Europe' features a cute 'dirty-old-man-but-not-really' figure who seems like he'd be fun when both parties are in the right mood for some mostly harmless yet inappropriate conversation. This class is basically a historical and cultural examination of the EU. 'Economic and political integration in the European Union' is, as best as I can tell, pretty much the same thing, with a younger, more French perspective. My placement in a language class was determined by a big test we all took during the adjustment week. I placed into the very highest level they offer -thanks to a good essay- where the average score is a whopping mid 60s out of 100. I only made it by about two points too, but I'm still gonna consider me a badass :) The prof. is a hoot. 'Strategic issues in key European industries'

has yet to meet and now isn't supposed to for a few weeks yet, some sort of planning confusion that no one seems to be too concerned about. Things are a lot looser here (not slack though, just loose). The professor is a member of the business community with lots of pertinent experience, so I'm excited to hear what he was to say.

All in all, they seem like good, caring people. I don't think we deserve them (I'm told French students tend to exhibit poor in-class behavior by U.S. standards, but so far this group is fitting right in).

Cell Phone:
Like I said, resistance was futile; I finally bought the cheapest cell phone I could find. It is my first one. Just as I feared, I was assimilated immediately after opening the box -tubes, nanoprobes, robotic implants everywhere, oh it was a huge mess. He's a cute little bugger though (not stylish enough to be the other gender I'd say). I'm going to call him Hugh [I bet about two of you will get all these Star Trek references]. After the fun of figuring out the whole service plan deal in French (Orange prepaid) at the store upstairs, I went down to the Carrefour to get an earpiece that could be objectively qualified without using the S-Word, unlike the one that came with it, and a carrying case. For that last element, I decided on a child's mitten (two laced together so they won't get lost, one for the phone and the other for the earpiece). It's indescribably cute. The phone is a Phillips candybar-style, and when I push the right buttons it uses first person personal pronouns *in the singular!* [Star Trek TNG: *'Descent'*, parts I and II -check it out!].
Cheerio,
    -Carl

Subject: **Phone Addendum**
Date: **Tuesday, 7 Feb 2006, 12:08**

See? It's already running my life...

France's dialing in code is 33, and that supplants the first 0 in my number (all French cells start with '06').

To call my cell from another cell from just about anywhere: +336.77.64.80.20 (if that's a local call it shouldn't be charged as long distance, even if dialed as such, assuming that's even a concern, I really don't know). The '+' in a cell phone is automatically replaced with the appropriate dialing-out code, I think.

To call from a non-France land line you need to dial a code to get out of that country as well as the '33' to get into this one-
To call from the US: 001-336-77-64-80-20
To call from pretty much anywhere in Europe: 00.336.77.64.80.20

All of this is of course provisional since I've never tried it to see if it works, plus there's the fact that the world's phone system is haunted by mischievous trolls, so nothing's for certain anyway. Sometimes leading zeros need to be left off, sometimes only with calling cards, sometimes not at all. Ask the trolls.

http://www.countrycallingcodes.com/

In summary: Yay e-mail :)

Subject: **'International incident'**
Date: **Wednesday, 15 Feb 2006, 07:43**

-if I was cool that phrase would be necessary to describe my time here. Alas....

Fast track:

Went to a disco- proved prominent theory of white man dancing.
Watched *Family Guy* DVDs with former French exchange student who lived in Juneau -shot of American culture greatly appreciated, giggity-gigity-goo.
Friend from home visited -feel fabulously melancholy.
Visited ancient nearby city -touched buildings old enough to be considered cool, thereby transferring coolness to self.

Familial guilt track:

General:
Reputable sources tell me that the French IRS, in order to accommodate the French tendency to buck rules *and* be secretive, automatically adds 10% to all statements of income, so if you *don't* cheat; you're screwed.

There are 7 McDonald's locations in Dijon. Despite the well-publicized objections, MacDo is very popular here. The fries don't taste right though [don't worry, I only had 1]

Recent-ish-ly-erected non-load-bearing walls in residential buildings are made with thinner Sheetrock here (in general, not just because of the different measuring systems). Then there's a sheet of crumbly Styrofoam, and then mortar and very thin-walled cubic cylinders made out of brown clay all stacked up. Finding a stud to hang things on is not easy, but the French seem to have a way.

You have to wonder how a nation's system of measurement has affected its history and economy. You can save a lot of money by rounding a measurement to two centimeters instead of an inch. But armor rounded to a half inch would be much better than a centimeter. How many nations have succeeded or failed on such small measurement details? What sort of differences have such things made throughout history? Gotta wonder...

The most prominent feature on the ubiquitous signs on the sterns of buses warning of wide turns and asking for courtesy when merging isn't the message itself, it's the line underneath stating which subparagraph of which page of which local and federal ordinances require drivers to give way. I think the idea of Common Law would make heads explode over here. The whole attitude seems off. If there's any sort of problem at all, a whole new law is created to address it, usually by *banning* something. These laws are frequently contradictory. Lawyers are hired to find ways to circumvent laws or discover a loophole, not to argue a lack of culpability based on evidence. In the end there are so many statutes that people are simply forced to ignore them to get through the day (though some laws are ignored deliberately; smoking in public places is, believe it or not, illegal, but you sure can't tell). The disillusioned say that the useless laws weaken the necessary ones.

Dijonaise friend-
It turns out Cécile, who lived in Juneau for a year in high school, goes to school in Dijon, and even saw me when I first arrived here and was appropriately astounded, but not quite sure enough that it was me to say hi at the time (makes sense, I'm supposed to be on another continent). After meeting up the other day we walked around the city in the rain and then ate at a Kebab place (vaguely Greek junkfood resembling a burrito sandwich comprised of meat shaved off of one of those massive, vertical, compressed meat-flake spindles dribbling grease as it rotates in a rotisserie apparatus). It looks great, but I was unimpressed. Then we went and watched the *'Family Guy'* movie and it was wonderful. It's great to know someone here, especially a person with such great taste in films.

Disco-

So the other night I left the house at 11:30PM with the intention of meeting someone at a bar for ten minutes and then being in bed before midnight. I came home at 5AM.

After a fun time at the bar chatting with several Frenchies who were an absolute delight, it closed, at which point they announced that we were going to some place called *Europia*. I wasn't really up for it, but I've been on this 'only one way to know what the right decision would have been' kick recently and I decided to go for it.

So a really cool French guy and girl, myself, the other American, and the Français who had been hitting on her all night and I all piled into a car and drove quite a ways out into the suburbs, eventually parking near a large building complex that was emanating earth-shaking bass notes.

We left all our coats and such in the car to avoid the checking fee and braved the freezing weather to get to the front door where we were patted down for alcohol and weapons, and then ushered into a vaguely Romanesque-looking lobby area with several halls leading away in different directions towards the various sins on offer.

As we came to the end of the hallway our fearless leader had chosen my first thought was "sacre merde, these places actually exist?!" The room was massive -a wide-open geometric dome ceiling covering a large dancing platform bathed in mist, lights, and lasers. There was a huge staircase leading up to an observation ring a story above the dance floor, both full to the brim, and this was surrounded by a sprawling, organically-shaped lounge area and a giant bar. Oh, and go-go cages. Oh yes. It was grand.

It was fun to dance without caring (the concept of being in a different zip code so it's okay applies very strongly here). It was also fun to watch the guys work their magic. Latin culture seems to be an odd mix of thick-headed outgoingness and crippling self-consciousness. The girls, as the song goes, just wanted to have fun.

The floor for the bathroom anteroom was tiled and had a ramp, all with lots of sweat condensed on it. It was fun to slide around Fred Flintstone style. Made for an impressive reentrance to the dance floor.

The lowest roof beams in the dome covered entirely too large a span for their size. A good snow and then rain could cause a lot of damage someday.

The whole night long I couldn't help but look at the crowd of several hundred people and think "Each person here paid five Euros to get in and then at least another ten for drinks every two hours, probably more." Holy cats.

Friend from Juneau and ancient village-
Bianca, who's been all over Europe the last few years, came to visit for two days. Dijon isn't nearly as cool as some of the places she's seen so far but I did get to give her an exciting tour involving all the dog crap on the sidewalks and an alley where some guys were dropping eggs from rooftops onto passing pedestrians. We had a great time :)

Her visit coincided with an ESCD bus trip to the city of Autun -the modern corruption of "*Augustodunum*." This is where Gaul was finally conquered by the Romans, and where Caesar spent a year writing his book about it afterwards. The town features some great stuff, including city gates that were once traversed by the emperor himself (and now by our bus-load of American tourists, how cool is that).

There is also an amphitheater that is supposedly 'the largest in the western part of the Empire' (a little vague) that could hold an audience of 15,000. Not much is left of the vertical structures thanks to time and progress (i.e. erosion and all the houses nearby which are made out of suspiciously Roman-looking rocks), but it still works just fine. I have a Bigfoot-Walking-Through-the-Forest quality still camera video of me "singing" 'I'm the Real Slim Shady' down in the focus. Fortunately most of the audio is obscured by Bianca laughing at me, so it's actually somewhat watchable.

We also saw a neat downtown area and a cathedral with an unbelievable quantity of bird droppings on the front steps. It would have been easier to just build a new door rather than try to clean it all up. It was truly amazing. I took a picture. The cathedral was fairly impressive too.

My address works! -but I think I'll change one thing on it: Programme U.S. -> Programme IES

Carl Brodersen
Programme IES
ESCDijon
29 rue Sambin
21000 Dijon
FRANCE

Cool.

Next week is vacations; I'm going to Switzerland. If I can I'll open a bank account.
        -Carl

ick.jpg

Subject: **Multinational generalizations**
Date: **Monday, 27 Feb 2006, 18:06**

Fast track:

Went to Switzerland -Finally; a nation with a currency that respects the American Empire [nationwide 20%-off sale]. Nice place.

Too much free time track:

Swiss vacation:
The first of the two one-week breaks I'll have here was just spent in western Switzerland (Fribourg) with Whitman buddy Nick who kinda lives there now in a wacky *dual-citizenship / his girlfriend is Swiss- so there you go,* sort of way.

Switzerland struck me as being far more progressive than the parts of France I've seen so far. Infrastructure was much more modern and helpful –the cities were there for their people, not to act as history sponges. The sidewalks were clear of dog doo, the buildings were very well kept up, and most everything was constructed out of very classy olive green sandstone that was orderly and in excellent shape. There was a lot of graffiti though, both paint and etchings in the soft stone. I guess there's a pretty big drug problem too. In some ways Switzerland struck me as a country set for a rude awakening at some point in the future. Much of Europe gives me this impression actually; as though there is a façade of past glory and current pleasantness that will melt (or be thrown off) when the old systems are finally confronted by a more open and changeable world that actually involves non-whites who aren't some kind of Christian.

The churches in Switzerland were exceptional. They were heated, very well lit, and under constant renovation. Moreover, they were wired for sound, wheelchair accessible, and many featured art created just in the last few years.

The best stained glass I've seen yet was the window work of the cathedral in Fribourg that was all commissioned quite recently and done by a local artist. In France they never seem to repair anything, for fear of losing historically important grime I guess. Again, structures for people here, not history. Standing at the corner by Nick's dorm, six of those tall yellow construction cranes could be seen, that gives you a pretty good idea of the amount of progress. Out with the old, in with the new that looks old.

I tried kabobs again (those Turkish shaved meat Greek jyro-like sandwich wraps) and they were orders of magnitude better. The most apparent difference was that the meat was ground more finely so it was more difficult to tell what you were eating, which is a good thing when it comes to kabobs.

Geneva was a hoot. We spent a lot of time at a church that had its crypt turned into an archaeological site with an audio tour. It's amazing what lies under old cities. There were at least three distinct churches on the site at one point or other, as well as other structures dating back to pre-Roman times. One can bet that humans have been worshipping various unexplained phenomena on that site as far back as a lack of understanding nature goes for our species. I wonder what odd occurrence drew them there in the first place. The tour included ancient wells, frescoes, bones, generic artifacts, dusty things, rocks, all kinds of good stuff! Definitely worth the effort it took to talk our way past the 8 Swiss Franc entry fee (of which we only had 7 CHF after counting all our coins) -it's remarkable what a smile can do for you.

Fribourg is so far my favorite city. It features ample elevation changes and structures that give it enough levels to make it interesting (flat tends to be boring). I spent four and a half hours on a self-guided walking tour (Nick has school he actually has to study for during breaks, "doctor" or something like that) -and had a blast crossing bridges, traversing forests, going up hills, down hills, along the river, through the city gate and down the winding stairs. The best part was standing at a watchtower on the far end of town and looking past the river and ravine, across the city, to a large hill far in the distance, upon which was a lone tree. Making it my only goal in life, I spent a good hour and a half finding the path to it, which is hard to do when you don't know where you're going. Despite several setbacks along the way it was finally Mission Accomplished just as the flash card filled up and it got dark. The tree was ancient and droopy; the only thing that stood out in a barley field managed by monks, with a large wooden bench underneath. It would be a great place for lovers, or stringing-up horse thieves.

Bern was also a hoot. The capital is very pretty, and we got to see the famous bears plodding around in their pit, which was too small, but well-furnished. And our timing was great- we got to take some interesting pictures of one pair "enjoying" themselves (the female seemed much less interested than the male; kind of uninterestedly scratching the ground in front of her with her claws, and both were less interested in it than the busload of Japanese tourists that arrived just as we did, some of whom were filming *and* snapping photos at the same time).

Had a fondue night and ate way too much for dinner. I attempted to make a cake that I like from back home, but with every single ingredient not quite what I had in mind it was a bit off. I was the only person who finished their one-sixth portion. It was good, but I won't begrudge the others their polite "I'm too full"s.

Watched a lot of hockey, and played a bunch as well. In Bern we went to an outdoor rink and got into a great Tough Hero state of mind when it started to rain but we kept on playing through in the torrential darkness, imagining somehow that admirers and future lady friends could somehow see us being so cool and studly, all with high school dance music coming in over the PA system. It was grand. We played several games with kids over the week I was there, all of which were a blast, even though they tended to be better than us (well, better than me at any rate, Nick actually knows what he's doing- "Carl, Alter, das kleine Mädchen hat dich voll am arsch gelegt").

Tried a tiny bite of chocolate for the first time in eight years (allergies suck). It was some fancy variety of exquisite quality so it seemed worth the attempt, but in retrospect I'd still rather just have a brownie.

Don't get Mexican food in Switzerland; they do the quantities wrong and not in the direction that allows one to be a happy hog. It's like they wanted you to eat healthy or something.

Still reeling from the disappointment of the "Mexican" place and in accordance with personal tradition, we had a nacho night with the best European ingredients we could find. Sadly, no UK or Swedish import stores were within walking distance so we had to make due without cheddar cheese (not an easy task let me tell you). Emmenthaler is the best substitute but it doesn't melt properly. And we had to use round chips, and ham. This place clearly needs a larger Hispanic population to support my dietary needs.

General Swiss:
Saw buildings being made of large 'bricks' that had honeycombed interiors to cut down on weight and heat loss. Great idea, but clearly this place is not expecting any earthquakes in the near future.

The minimum initial deposit for foreigners opening secret Swiss bank accounts is $20,500 with an up-front service fee of around $700. Oy.

Points of interest:
Practically every vehicle I've seen in Europe has had side-mirrors that fold in.

International Generalizations

Am currently recovering from some sort of flue/chest cold that Nick had better not get or I'll feel really guilty and will blame him for making me feel bad. Being sick is no fun, especially while traveling (in this case the upside was an ample supply of cheap Ricola during the worst phase).

It was nice to get back to Dijon in the end. I've settled here to some degree, so it was a bit like a home-coming, which was nice, though honestly - I feel ready to go someplace again already ("bzzzzz, travelbug, bzzzzz").

And now it's time for homework that didn't happen over the break, more naps, lots of water, and an early bedtime.
    -Carl

Subject: **Stereogeneraltypeization, in full 5.1 surround!**
Date: **Friday, 3 Mar 2006, 18:27**

Fast track:

Made lasagna for first time ever as part of intense culinary adventure -no explosions reported, but locals still tense. Day one of new internship at local bank = how many different ways can I think of to say *"Welcome! The person over there will actually know how to help you!"*

Ze other track:

Finally Used the Oven at Home:
So you know that scene in '*Castaway*' where Tom Hanks' character has made his continued survival possible by lighting a fire after much effort, and he stands in awe of it on the beach, proclaiming his victory to the darkness with primal caveman-like pride? Imagine me doing that, except it was "*I*, have-made-Lasagna!" Yes, I'm very proud of myself. It's good too, though it's worth mentioning that baked Emmenthaler cheese has the consistency of press-board once it dries, so watch out for that. We all know Cheddar would be preferable of course, but then so would a shower head that's actually attached to the wall. Also, make sure you buy *pitted* olives over here, it turns out the can I bought was the least expensive for a reason.... (To remove the pit from an olive not intended for presentation purposes, squish it between thumb and forefinger joint. Cutting them open individually takes way too long.)

Carrefour Adventures:
When shopping for Lasagna ingredients I discovered Brand-X peanut butter in the foreign foods aisle!!! (it's very rare here). Of course it wasn't chunky Adams Natural, and is better described as 'peanut *paste*,' but the PB&J with honey I made was still orgasmic.

Language:
The main reason I chose this program was that it was the

only one available to me that offered classes Whitman's Econ. department would accept for credit towards my degree (at about a 4:1 exchange rate) -allowing me to actually graduate on time. It seems that a lot (not all, but a lot) of the other U.S. students here came because there's no language requirement (meaning most of the classes are in English).

Since I didn't have much of a choice at the time, I didn't really think about the implications of there being no requirement, but now that I'm here, I don't think I'd recommend a program like this is English is your first language. For starters, English being as dominant as it is, you gotta question the motives (read: "coolness") of an Anglophone who chooses a language program with no language requirement (it's real easy to get by on the linguistic talents of others, but who wants to spend time with folks that lazy?) Second; I am, of course, not learning French anywhere near as quickly as I'd like. Alas.

The upside is that I'm getting what is probably an above average international student experience (meaning great exposure to non-U.S.ies in addition to the Frenchies). But we all speak English when we're hanging out since that's everybody's best second language. This means that I have an awkward leg up on all my friends in the communication department. I can be a useful source of clarification now and then, but I always have to watch myself to not be "the expert." There are a few in our group who can speak French as well or better than I can, so I always do my best to speak French with them when the situation allows, but not if that would exclude somebody from the conversation. I guess our priority is contact, not language.

Internship:
I described my interests to the school's job placement committee as being generally oriented towards art and creativity, with a special appreciation for information technology, being outdoors, and a fondness of children and teaching, -so they put me in a bank.

It's okay though- it's entirely in French, and also an opportunity to observe the culture, so I'm fine with their selection (this specific rationale is very convenient and can be used to justify anything from excessive TV viewing, to tabloid reading, to nights spent in the local jail). I'll spend two half days a week in different positions at a very old bank in the heart of the city (it's actually a "caisse" [*cache, stash*] which means it's really more of a 'Financial Institution' than just a bank per se, or so they keep insisting). My particular branch is very well established and nicely built, a good mix of old and new styles. The logo (it took me a whole day of staring at it to figure it out) is a squirrel. I work at Squirrel Bank. I guess the allusion is that their customers are like small rodents stashing nuts in a tree.

Today they had me observe (for five minutes) and then *run* the front desk, which faces straight out the glass front door. My job was to not make eye contact with incoming customers too early so as to not create an awkward situation while we both had to wait for them to come within speaking range; to, on arrival, let them explain briefly what their desires were and perhaps hand me a piece of paper; to look at said paper as though I knew what was going on; and to then politely direct them across the way to where the lady who actually speaks French will be able to assist them, thank you and have a nice day. Any time the phone rang I would smile at it and refuse to feel threatened (I decided that since I wouldn't understand, wouldn't know the answer, and didn't know how to transfer calls, that it was best to let the messagerie get it).

It's a bit of a bummer, since I know that if I had the proper degree of fluency I'd be able to charm the socks off everyone who comes into that place- even without knowing anything in the way of useful information: "Well Madam my first inclination is to say that you're absolutely right but I must admit to being a bit new here and I want to be certain I don't misinform you so I'm going to direct you just over there to Elise if you don't mind as I'm sure she'll be able to get you that answer right away, thank you very much and have a super day, oh and here, I believe these are yours?" [hands customer her socks].

I had to buy a shirt and tie since the hobo banker look isn't very popular over here. I went with a lavender shirt. The branch director was the only other guy in the whole place that wasn't wearing a generic white chemise. Betcha I own the place in a few months.

I've finally decided to take action against the French dog doo problem. I'm going to start photographing it. No wait, hear me out; I'll make a poster-sized collage that is a map of France made of dog crap. This will be sent to the already anti-poo mayor of Dijon in the hopes that it can be used to gain support for the drive against droppings (if only people knew how others saw France…). Laziness is one thing, but national pride is another. Plus it'd be funny as hell.

Cheers!
    -Carl

Subject: **It's snowing in Belgium, but only a little**
Date: **Saturday, 11 Mar 2006, 15:28**

Fast track:

Went to a fancy Italian opera, culture now coming out the wazoo[1].
Waffles baby, yeah! (Belgium trip)
-Confirmed existence of EU.
Well into 'that's just gross' stage of recovery from flu bug.

"Good lord this is long…" track:

Opera and city planning:
Dijon has one of the newest and nicest theater halls in France, and a group of us students went to see *LaTraviata* there last weekend. "Traviata" is an Italian word meaning "main character falls in love and then spends an hour dying at the top of her lungs." As well as the delightful singing I especially enjoyed the special effects. Several scenes called for inclement weather, and so they actually had water sprayed down onto the stage. Using water to simulate rain –genius!

Our seats weren't the best (each came with altitude sickness pills and an oxygen canister) but we were lucky to get them at all. The trip was organized by the culture class professor, who has a remarkable ability to put up with American students. It was a hoot, and we're lucky we had him as a guide.

The theater building itself is shaped like a piano, with the main body held aloft by three giant pillars, and all the spiral stairs to get up to it are bloody backwards. It was constructed during the term of a now former mayor who was oddly progressive in terms of new construction projects (which is probably why they canned him).

---

[1] For a scientific discussion of the Wazoo, see 'Gray's Anatomy of the Human Body' (I forget which page, but just check the index).

There is actually a fair amount of construction and expansion going on in Dijon, left over from when said mayor was in office, but in terms of available space the city has pretty much reached its maximum area of coverage; it now borders protected or unusable land on all sides. Any new change will have to come from within, at the cost of whatever is replaced by the new. *gasp!*

Mayors are far more important here. We have the word "presidency", but no single word to match "mayor-time", which is one of the connotations of *mairie*. They're like local kings, and all seem to have a Versailles Complex when it comes to urban renewal and leaving their mark on the town.

Game show dichotomy:
French television presents two extremes when it comes to game shows. On the one end they have tripe so bad it makes "Who Wants to be a Millionaire?" seem sophisticated and well-written, and on the other they have programs that, for example, revolve around contestants solving anagrams and playing deductive math games – in one they're given six numbers to manipulate with basic arithmetic functions and a target number (the audience quietly plays along too), all set to light piano music.

Feeling better:
I'm finally at the last stage of being sick: spending a few days clearing my lungs out. It's been thrilling. It occurred to me while boiling a dried soup packet one afternoon that the advertisements on the package could describe quite well certain aspects of my decongesting process: "Zesty", "Family-sized", "With real chunks of beef", "25% more, *free*!" and so on.

Toys "R"<- Us exists here:
Enamel paint for plastic models comes in cute little paint cans -in the U.S. we just have tiny glass jars.

There was a neat game on display where you could use a toy revolver to shoot plastic cans off a plastic log. I noticed that of the four of us who were there, the two Finns and I were great shots, but the Belgian guy didn't even know how to hold the gun. I learned later that both of the Finns (now in their mid 20s) were such good shots because they had high-ish military ranks, had each commanded a reserve platoon, and knew how to use guns up to an AK-47 because Finland has compulsory military service (a fair number of European countries do, or a longer civil-service alternative like in Germany). I guess that explains it.
So what's my excuse?

End of the lasagna:
I finally finished the lasagna I made so many days ago. In a delightfully Shelley-esque turn of events, I found by the end of eating it day after day that I had come to loathe my creation –lamenting whatever unnatural urge had led me to even consider its making in the first place. But once gone, I came to sorely miss its presence and regretted my desire that it should be no more. Also it killed a friend of mine (there were noodles just everywhere….).

Guardrails-
-so far have the same general structure for the bumper part as seen in the U.S., but the support posts are significantly more feeble. In the U.S. we have those beefy, six-inch galvanized I-beams holding them up. Here there are widely spaced poles that look like they belong in a chain link fence. I guess if you're not stopping fat SUVs…

Cement trucks-
-have a slightly larger capacity than the U.S. standard; the mixing drum is thinner, but significantly longer.

Semi trucks:
Every cargo truck I've seen looks quite new, and is the type where the cab rests on top of the engine (the front is completely flat) -probably so they're as short as possible for

the small roads. They all appear to have very clean-running engines and fancy filter systems. They also have all had in the back three axles each with two extra-wide tires on each one —no twosies.

Swiss again:
I think I forgot to mention earlier that the Swiss made impressive use of metal flashing in their construction. There were lots of copper roofs, and many buildings featured stainless steel seals along corners and edges.

The finger
-is less of a big deal here, to the point that you really have to scowl and shake your hand to get it across that you're telling a person to go fornicate with themself. As such, it's common for people to use it as their primary pointing finger rather than the index finger. I wonder if we'd do that too if it wasn't so loaded with meaning (perhaps its natural usability was why it was selected for the purpose in the first place).

Pop [or "soda," if you insist, but not "coke," that's a brand]:
I'm pretty sure the walls of aluminum cans are thicker in Europe. I wonder what the extra cost is for that, and if that's a units of measure issue or a specific desire (maybe they make them thinner in the U.S. to facilitate crushing against the forehead).

Passing lanes:
Europeans will drive in the right lane whenever possible. Any and all left lanes are for passing only, and even when passing two cars only a little ways apart, the passer will pull back into the right while between them, even if they're only going to rest there for three seconds before pulling out again to take the second car. I realized today, watching cars whiz by our bus to Brussels, that this is actually an incredibly efficient system. It prevents the formation of a 'front' that blocks everyone behind and clots the road, and keeps weaving from happening (I imagine leaping would be just slightly less dangerous?). It's really a good system.

Socialist Failures and inner moral struggle:
The other day three of us were walking through a busy market downtown when we were handed a newspaper/ brochure by a vaguely eastern-looking woman, quite out of the blue. We had no idea what it was for, even after asking and getting an explanation that we couldn't understand, so we just thanked her and started to leave –at which point communication suddenly became easy (funny that), and she said that our new papers were 'for the children' and cost six Euros. With the exchange rate that's like U.S. $1million, so we said 'no thank you' and gave them back. Then I gave her the three Euros worth of large coins I had on me and said 'good luck.' But, even when with that done, and despite my charming smile[2], her hand, still holding the 3€, didn't move from its outstretched position. Instead of thanking us for the *donation* she just looked at us with her best sob story face and kept repeating that it was 'for the children' in the most pitiable voice I've heard in a while. I tried to explain the concept that I had already given her something and that was all for us, but it didn't work. In the end we just had to walk away, which I find difficult to do. Of course not once did we get a "*merci*." It was annoying that there was no appreciation at all, and it really made me think about my own experiences with charity work where the roles were reversed (I'm convinced politeness gets more than the hard sell).

Anyway, in the following week I ran into them again and the same thankless, guilt-inducing tactics were used once more. When asked the second time I said I had no money because that's more polite than an outright 'no' of course, but they know how to hook people who can't say 'no' and persisted, choosing to see a lie instead of politeness. This second time I got rather annoyed and just ignored them instead of trying to be polite, feeling righteous and loathsome at the same time. Why should I deprive kids just

---

[2] seriously, *what* ego?

because their benefactors were rude? Why should I give them anything at all? If I want to, how much is enough? Can a lie be a good thing? Were there really any "children" at all? I worry too much.

I continued down the street with my undeclared spare change, mulling the experience over, until I happened past a guy playing an accordion. I stopped to listen for a nice moment, then dropped my last 1 Euro coin into his hat. He smiled and thanked me. I thanked him for his music and wished him a nice day. He nodded back.

At the start of the Belgium trip, on the bus very early in the morning, I saw a homeless guy in the foyer of Squirrel Bank (which is left open to allow access to the ATM during off hours). He was on the steps in front of the locked door to the inner part of the building, to the left of the ATM, sleeping rolled up the welcome mat. It was a powerful mixture of images. Never take for granted the comforts you have in life.

Awesome fun trip to Belgium, yay fun:
(-This part is much less gloomy-)
I don't feel as bad attributing my observations of one city to an entire nation in the case of Belgium, because from a surface-area standpoint I'm much more likely to be right.

In general, Brussels is great. I'm definitely coming back here with my dad for our European tour [Dad; we're going to Brussels, cool? Sweet]. This part-of-the-package official bus trip is comprised of students from several of the exchange programs at the ESCD, not just the U.S. program, and is the first time they've really mixed with each other in an official way. Part of this lack of interaction is a result of the other exchange students being older and in different classes (most are working on a their masters degree equivalents), but I'm still surprised at how little the Americans are interested in them. They all sat together on the bus and generally kept to themselves throughout the trip, despite comments from the others that it was so nice to finally be doing things together and that the groups should hang out more. It amazes me that the two social groups that have developed are a multinational one with people from fifteen different countries who are all in different programs, and an American one.

Architecture:
It's newer (there's nothing for urban renewal like 1,000 years of other European countries settling their differences in your backyard). The houses still have the same basic theme as the rest of Europe, but they're better built and more efficient, and they don't reflect as many forced adaptations to silly French taxation laws that made you pay the government for each window, and I have yet to see any Mansard roofs (the Mansard is technically an attic, so *story taxes* didn't apply to that level of the house -they're a clever lot those Parisians).

Cars:
The city was clearly built for them. Here they are larger and more prevalent than the tiny Renaults and SmartCars zipping around the streets in Dijon (many of which were built for horses). I'd like to see a study relating 'overall modernity' to average car size.

EU headquarters:
We've toured several large, new-looking EU buildings since arriving, and it was all very impressive. The European Union is a supranatural body born of the battlefields of this continent, conceived to make future wars unthinkable by pouring such a large proportion of each member nation's GDP into the creation of fancy brochure dossiers for visitors that there simply isn't enough left over to pay for a conflict (seriously, all forty of us each got a packet that was an inch thick). So far the scheme is working splendidly, and all those color images on A4 heavy gloss look great (by the way EU, thanks for letting me take two).

Food:
-Waffles; oh yes, oh yes indeedy.
-Beer; tasted great, best three sips I've ever had.
-Chocolate; sure looks nice...

Texmex restaurant - "*holy crap they serve quesadillas!*":
Yes, I finally found a place with cheddar cheese. That should tide me over for another three months.

Teensy alley full of restaurants (tables indoors and out):
There was a thin but unbelievably long alleyway packed to the gills with eateries near the city center. It was really cool, but the food looked better than it tasted. I bet in looking at distance from the two entrances one could make a nifty study about pricing and advertisement techniques, especially back when the place first filled up and new innovations and competition were developing. Each restaurant has a door jockey that tries to hook passers-by, rather like fisherman at a hatchery trying to snag salmon. I was very much enamored with the place and wanted to come back and try each one, but it turned out there are seventy-five of them. I might not make it to them all....

Numbers:
The French number system is ridiculous. Going by tens, after sixty there's "sixty-ten," "four-twentys," "four-twentys-ten," and 99 is "four-twentys-ten-nine" (quatre-vingt dix-neuf). But! when I asked a 'fisherman' about how many restaurants there are in the alley he said *septant-cinq* (seventy-five), instead of the high French *soixant-quinze* (sixty-fifteen). Yay! Same improvement for ninety, but eighty is still four twenties. 20 was important to the ancient Gauls and Celts, I'm told, so it remains still today, even if the Belgians modernized the rest.

The hotel breakfast buffet serves pâté. How ritzy is that? The hotel also has wireless (clearly), so life is good.
Toodle-oo!
    -Carl

Subject: **Bruxelles part II**
Date: **Friday, 17 Mar 2006, 13:54**

Fast track:

More random musings and things noticed.
Photo!!!
Made it back to Dijon.
Still alive.

***"Dude, seriously, when do you, like, go outside and stuff?"* track*:*

This finishes off the trip to Belgium and ties up a few other lose ends. Hope everyone is well.

General Belgium:
Traffic:
The main avenues all have tunnels that bypass intersections with perpendicular streets by dropping down from street level to go right under them and then come back up to street level, and all the turning is done from side lanes that parallel the main drag until the intersection, so only those making turns need concern themselves with the process, and everyone else can have a good time dolphining along like Skipper. The ramps leading back up after the underpasses were pretty steep too; I bet you could get air if you really tried ("Aight! on three; everybody run to the back of the bus!!").

Some streets have in their medians small (two-car) trams that run on rails level with the pavement. This provides the temptation to use this area as a left turn lane if the sanctioned lane is full of traffic (and if no trams are coming). We saw a guy do this while we were waiting to turn right. He jerked out onto the rails and sped up towards the intersection to make his left, only to come to a screeching halt when a cop car that was waiting forty vehicles in front of him pulled out to block his way. The officer scolded the driver and then drove off. Three other cars successfully pulled the same move before we made it past the intersection.

Giant funky building:
Belgium has a park with a large building called the Atomium that is made of LARGE spheres and cylinders that form the shape of a cube (spheres at the corners, cylinders connecting them, all balanced on one corner, with a central sphere suspended in the middle by cylinders protruding inwards from each of the corner spheres, so all told each corner sphere has four cylinders connected to it). The line to get up to the top for a view was too long, so I'll defer to the next time I'm in Belgium, but it was fun to look at. They claim it was built for the World's Fair, but I'm pretty sure that was just a cover, and that it actually houses some sort of sinister, planet-crushing laser device [see photo].

The Atomium is near an exhibition hall that was running a home show while we visited. As a result, we got stuck in the worst case of gridlock I've ever seen. We waited at one intersection for almost ten minutes for a path to open up amid the tangled nest of cars that had clogged it, and even then only made it through because of some significant vehicular shifting in the middle to give us room with an inch of clearance on each side. In the dead center of all the trapped cars was a guy with a shining new Alfa Romeo, unable to move -with SUVs and tour buses squeezing by him in all directions. I think I could hear his heartbeat when we went by.

Visit to Brugge:
Brugge is the Venice of Belgium, located in the "Dutch" speaking part of the country -which has a language fantastically similar to German (a citizen from one could say that the language of the other is a mispronunciation of his/her own). Of course everyone spoke English too, sadly. And the dislike of the Dutch part of Belgium for the French part of Belgium being what it is, you're better off just opening with English.

The city is surrounded by a canal on three and a half sides and bisected by another. It was a very cute, very touristy town. We bused over for a day and had a good time shopping and wondering about. I ditched the Americans at the beginning for a few hours of wandering, and then met up with the non-French international students.

Brugge is famous for a hill with windmills on it- we surmised at the end of the trip after noticing a certain pattern among the items in the gift shops. With only an hour before we had to be back at the bus, we decided that we would all die right then and there if we didn't get to see it, and committed ourselves body and soul to finding the hill. With a poorly xeroxed map as our only guide, we only had time for one shot at guessing where to go, and ended up running all-out through the streets (in what turned out to be the right direction) at long last and with the clock ticking finding a large (I'm guessing artificial) hill by a river with several very old windmills historically preserved on it. This was a great victory for all of us, and many pictures were taken. Appropriately, there was a farm of those massive, modern windmills in the distance, providing an excellent image of old and new. I ended up hyper-extending my knee on the mad rush to get back though, and am only now walking normally again, but pain lets you know you're alive, or something macho like that.

Hotel:
As mentioned, the complimentary breakfast included pâté - which is gross, but classy. Europeans know how to live. And the shower had good pressure, lots of hot, was easily adjustable, and above all, the head was attached to the wall. Paradise.

Belgian toilet paper comes in units of almost the same distance across as in France, but are about half and inch longer. French toilet paper has the same rough proportions as U.S. toilet paper, but is about 1/4 inch smaller all around. Swiss toilet paper was longer than the French, but shorter than the Belgian, and still smaller than the US's. Oh how I do love travel.

Cheese:
That's right, *I found cheddar cheese for sale in a store!!*[3] It's British, and thus not Tilamook®, but by golly it's orange cheese! I was inspired to look after finding it in that restaurant, and lo and behold there it was, wreathed in rose petals and shining like the sun, cherubs harping nearby. I took it home with me, and yesterday made avocado grilled cheese sandwiches. It didn't melt quite the right way (too gooey and ductile) but it was gooooood. Soon there will also be quesadillas, tacos, and steamed broccoli à la cheese melted on top. It's been a good week for this reason alone (even though an eight-pack of flour tortillas cost me the equivalent of about $4.50 because the market's just too small).

Back in France:
My dog crap art project that requires many photos of said deposits is advancing well (come on, when do I ever joke about projects?). Sometimes I get to know my subjects even, having charted their locations and characteristics, carefully remembering each one so as to not repeat (no doubles, this piece has to have integrity). You get to know them after a while; "I wonder if the stringy on rue du Nord has caught anybody yet...." I feel like Galileo and his stars... except with little piles of dog crap and probably fewer ramifications for humanity on the whole.

They have the word "*Internaute*" here to describe a web user -like *astronaut* or *cosmonaut*, and it appears to be in common use. I think this is delightful. ["*Taikonaut*," if you're wondering why I left it out, is actually a perfectly logical but unsanctioned term coined by Malaysian journalists. The Chinese word is completely different, and in official English translations the word 'astronaut' is used.]

---

[3] !! -!

International Generalizations

The people of Dijon seem to be willing to put absolutely anything out for the garbage trucks- huge piles of cardboard, lumber, office plants, even defunct Xerox machines. Even more astoundingly, everything has been picked up -except for the copier, which has been sitting next to a lamppost by the road for almost a month. I named him Rudy.

Tomorrow I'm heading up to Paris to meet a friend who's over for her spring break. We couldn't confirm anything due to scheduling difficulties, so plan A is to meet at the train station when I arrive, which I'm hoping will fall through so we can revert to plan B; the infinitely cooler *meet under the Eiffel tower at noon.* - yeah, life is good :)
Cheerio!

Automium.jpg

Subject: **Paris!**
Date: **Monday, 20 Mar 2006, 14:20**

Fast track:

Went to Paris.

Slightly less fast track:

Went to Paris [see humorous photo].
Met traveling friends from home.
Looked at stuff, took a boat ride and lots of pictures.
Loved it, plan to return.

"Good Lord, another one? Well at least you got some fresh air doing this..." track:

How to get to Paris:
Be up and smiling at the crack of 5AM.
Walk to station and board train, armed with 15-Euro Special Deal for Masochists ticket.
Arrive three hours later at personal nemesis Gare de Lyon, where confusing labeling led to forfeiture of painfully expensive ticket to Dijon during first visit...

...The place doesn't seem as foreboding as it did the first time around. My friend from Juneau, Tally, wasn't at the station, which meant falling back to the other two proposed but unconfirmed times later on (woohoo!) --so it was off to go exploring.

How to visit Paris:
Say to self "In the streets of Paris, wow! Let's find something famous and gawk at it!"
Look at map, walk for about five minutes.
Pause suddenly, look at direction of shadows on sidewalk, smack forehead and start walking in opposite direction.
Wish you hadn't smacked head so hard, it kind of hurts now... -until finally:
"Hey look a monument! Let the tourism begin!"
[Taking of photos commences.]

The first monument I came to was the monument at the Place de la Bastille, the everlasting and mystery-shrouded symbol of a nation's freedom, which featured some quality graffiti on its pedestal. In place of the famous prison that once stood there is now a massive pillar in the middle of a roundabout with a naked, golden nymph on top. Cheeky bugger that I am, I opted to take my photos from the 'cheeky' side.

From there I generally walked along the Seine, to the Eiffel Tower, up to the Arc de Triumph, and back again [Funny how when written in English one of those is in French and the other isn't].

The Seine is a large, muddy river, that while passing through Paris is entirely walled-in, with boat launches and steps that go right into the water and near-water-level walkways, with full public access to it all. I'd say the river was about three feet above normal when I was there, and it had a tremendous current.

Notre Dame is smaller than it looks in pictures, but still very impressive. It's on one of the two islands where the city began 2,000 years ago. The islands were natural occurrences at the time, but by now they're at the point where stone and mortar has made them entirely artificial. The cathedral itself, however, was created by receding glaciers at the end of the Pleistocene and is an entirely natural formation.

After that stop I came across some shiny fountain that I had never heard of and took several pictures of it, mostly because of peer pressure (the other tourists were all doing it and I wanted to be cool).

All along the Seine are large green boxes bolted to the tops of the short walls that line the river side of the sidewalks. They look like they might house lifejackets, but turned out to contain deployable markets for books and art that, at night, could be folded up and locked, which is a wonderfully efficient idea.

At nearly all points along my westward walk I could see tiny bits of the top of the Eiffel Tower peeking up over buildings, slowly revealing itself more and more, until a corner was turned and voila there it was!

The Eiffel tower is absolutely beautiful. Someday I'll make a model of it to accent my "Hey look I went to Europe and now I'm all cultured!" future home décor, such is the degree to which I'm now enamored with it. It deserves every bit of the fame that it has, and you should take special care in how you first see it because you'll never get that moment again. For maximum effect -the biggest 'bam!'- I recommend approaching from the northeast. Make this your first task in Paris so you don't see it accidentally (take the extra time to keep away from the Seine at first so the tower remains out of view). To start, head for the Arc de Triumph -don't actually go up there yet since the top of the tower will be visible, but from that general area find the Avenue Kléber (it's huge) and follow it southwest. It ends in a roundabout with a horse'n'hero statue and the back side of the Palais de Chaillot, which is made of two curved buildings forming a semicircle opening up towards the Tower with a large walkway in between them. Follow this walkway between the two wings of the palace and there, as you descend the stairs, will suddenly be the entirety of the grand tower, kerpow, all at once, backlit by the sun (there will also be several hundred Asian tourists taking pictures). Take the time to do this, it's the greatest photo-op in the world.

If you're going to meet someone under the tower be sure to specify which pylon -I picked North since it's the closest to Alaska. Dead center underneath is also an option - there's a metal utility box cover marking the spot (don't be fooled by the manhole cover you'll see first, it's a few feet off from the middle). Still no Tally when I arrived, so I sat and ate one of my sandwiches (yes, Carl goes to the capital of the most culinarily-prestigious country in the world and brings his own lunch), and then walked on to the end of the Champs de Mars. I had been hitting the Nalgene bottle pretty hard in a place where you have to pay to use the can, so this walk was important as the Champs de Mars features some of the only good tall bushes in the city, if you get my drift (brave guys and braver girls take note of this to save a Euro spending a penny).

The dirt used for filler and as a path topper in Paris looks like crushed sandstone, and is chock-full of tiny chunks of flint. Oh how important that substance once was to so many.... It certainly wasn't weapons grade material, but I examined a few pieces in awe anyway, kind of like a person a hundred years from now looking with bemused fascination at a chunk of Uranium he found on the sidewalk.

Next was the Arc de Triumph, built by Napoleon to honor the military and himself and not in that order. It stands at the end of the Champs Elysées, in the Étoile de Traffic Coming at You From all Directions at 100 Miles an Hour. [Jokes by Mark Russell and Dave Barry]. There are access tunnels under the traffic circle now, but getting to their entrances requires the crossing of multiple massive motorways, many manifest with multiple maniacal motorists (okay I'm done) which means standing on tiny mediums in the middle of a four lane highway with lots of other frightened tourists, waiting for the light to change. While you're there, try not to let tourist mode kick-in and wander into traffic to get a better angle, the people in the cars have seen it all and they might not bother swerving around you if their car hasn't been washed recently and needs to be taken in anyway.

The Arc de Triumph, Paris edition, is huge (much bigger than the one in Dijon –which for its size is more along the lines of an Arc de Success). I didn't climb up to the top, (again; cheapskate) but I did note with great satisfaction that the staircases all spiral in the right direction. After taking the requisite number of photographs to be allowed to leave the premises (there are cultural officers who will check your camera) I saluted the Unknown Soldier and headed back to the tower for the 3:00 meeting attempt.

On the way there a guy nailed me at 20 yards as an American and I got sucked into paying twenty Euros to have him draw a caricature of me. I'd always heard of these guys, so I figured what the heck, kitsch value (though I should have talked him down to ten, for the fifty cents in materials he spent that still would have represented a 2000% return on his investment which is not bad in today's market). At twenty Euros for eight minutes of effort plus let's say the fifteen minutes it takes to find a willing sucker this guy is making $52 an hour. I justified my purchase by having him sign it so I could track his career and then resell after he becomes famous.

The drawing is nice, though apparently it's time for a haircut.

Third time at the north pylon was a charm, so I can now say I've meet a lady in Paris under the Eiffel Tower. We also ran into another person on exchange from Juneau who just happened to be there. He said the he hadn't had any of his university classes in weeks due to strikes over new employment legislation called the CPE (First Employment Contract) that have been going on for weeks (he didn't seem to be too torn up about it).

With Tally and all the other people who were meeting her in Paris (friends from her school) I took a river ride on one of the many funky-looking tourist boats chugging up and down the Seine (which were running on a slightly altered course from usual due to the high water).

If you take a boat tour don't sit near the stern; the engines on these thing are not built for stealth.

It was wonderful to be back on the water again, I always miss it. The boats allowed great views of every-thing, especially the bridges. Some of their undersides showed that they had been expanded over time to meet the needs of traffic, and under some, large cracks showed where work would have to be done soon. In general they seemed to be in a good state or repair though.

The tour was guided by a friendly tape-recorder in a box that knew how to talk in four different languages. Our excursion took place during the day, but the tours run well into the night, and the boats have bank after bank of spotlights to illuminate all the sights in the dark. I can just imagine some frustrated near-river resident leaning over his balcony at midnight taking potshots at the bulbs with a .22 -protest is a way of life here.

One of the bridges, it was announced by the box, was special in that if it was your first time passing under it you had to kiss the person next to you or suffer dire consequences. The problem with it is that they tell you about this potentially critical juncture in your life about a hundred feet from the bridge, leaving precious little time to make the proper arrangements. I was fortunate in that I had a nice rosy cheek available (boy, Tally's a real trooper), but not all the first-timers were so lucky. I felt especially bad for the guy sitting on the same bench as a couple and their large sheep dog.

After the boat ride it was well past time to head back to the train station, so I took my leave of a still slightly shaken Tally and her friends and make haste for the Gare de lyon.

I avoided pedestrian traffic by running along the river, looking at a map trying to decide where I would want to cross. As I neared the bridge I had decided on, distinct but unintelligible chanting became audible, though no source of the voices was in view. Recalling news reports of the protests that had occurred over the last two days, I was able to guess at what probably lay ahead, taking into account also that the platoons of gas mask-wearing riot police I kept passing by probably weren't there to enjoy the sunset (which was lovely by the way).

Finally, late and really hurrying along now, my bridge came into view and sure enough it was covered by protesters chanting anti CPE slogans and waving banners. I pressed on, armed with my pointy umbrella and a resolve to not be foiled twice by the same gare. (At this point it bears mentioning that the march was still a march, and not the riot it became later that night when the civilizing force of women and children had left it to go to bed at a reasonable hour, so don't give me too much adventuring (or stupidity) credit.)

I ran out of time about three blocks from the station. The new ticket cost me forty Euros, but at least that way I got to ride on a TGV, which is much more comfortable that the cheap option, and so fast that I arrived in Dijon only eleven minutes late despite waiting over an hour in Paris for my new train (eleven is also the number of minutes I missed the first train by).

I found some high ground along a road outside the station and stood with curious Parisians watching the throngs of thousands pass underneath. It was a lot like a 4th of July parade back home, just with less blind patriotism and fewer interesting floats –and a slightly stronger socialist undertone than one is likely to see there. I talked with a guy next to me about what various signs meant and whether the protests could work (-force the annulment of the legislation, which has already been passed by the parliament). No one seems to know the answer to that big question. When the hour to my train had almost elapsed I decided to head to the platform early, so I thanked the guy for his conversation (after waiting four or five minutes for him to stop making out with his wife and come up for air –Parisians!) and hopped on the train.

So at the end of the day, Gare de Lyon had me at 0 for 2, but it was a fabulous time, and I'll definitely return. A minute at each painting in the Louvre takes four months - it's a year for the whole works) and there are plenty of other places I didn't see. For now though I have good memories, and great photos of the places I visited ("this is the line for Notre Dame, this one's the line for the Eiffel Tower, and here we have the line for the Arc"...). Tourism on the cheap, gotta love it (besides, this way I still have all sorts of new experiences to look forward to for future visits).

Overall, Paris struck me as a town that adored its past, but was equally in love with having a good image, so all the buildings were either kept up to modern standards or actually were modern- but in a classical way. I loved the feeling that the city belonged to its citizens and not as much to the government that resides there now. It was open, nothing was cordoned off, you could go anywhere, even the dangerous parts with water. I'm glad the U.S. isn't running things there, it would all be blocked off to escape liability in personal injury lawsuits.

May we meet someday in Paris,[4]
    -Carl

Footnote: Based on a scaled map and a piece of string, I walked just more than twenty-five kilometers during my nine-hour visit. I'm glad I ditched my "don't' hassle me I'm local" brown leather loafers for my "Why yes, I *do* happen to be a foreigner!" running shoes.

---

[4] The use of Clichés is only a misdemeanor here

International Generalizations

American in paris.jpg

Subject: **Howdy-do!**
Date: **Tuesday, 30 Mar 2006, 13:17**

Fast track:

More bus time; visited villages in neighboring region.
Political demonstrations = one heck of a party.
Cooking class 1 of 2: so much butter!

"The first two paragraphs are about light bulbs and hinges?!" track:

There are two kinds of light bulb hook-ups here; the standard threaded, and the original French version which is not screwed into the socket but rather pushed straight in and then locked by twisting ninety degrees –it has two pegs on either side of the business end that stick out perpendicular to the long axis of the bulb, which fit into grooves in the socket when inserted and rotated, holding the unit in place and lining-up the electrical connectors –which are both on the bottom end of the bulb, side by side.

Hinges here are different too, and in some ways are more secure. Instead of a series of interlocking vertical tubes attached to plates the door and frame with a pin holding them in line, there is usually just a bottom half attached to the frame with a vertical pin and a top half attached to the door that receives the pin. To remove a door entirely, all you have to do is open it and lift it up, but if it's closed, you're out of luck; the doorframe will be in the way (unlike in the U.S. where you can take the hinge pins out if you're on the right side of the door). The hinges themselves are screwed into the wood like a sideways corkscrew. Lining them up appears to be a pain, and may explain squeakiness, but the inability to remove a closed door from its hinges is certainly an advantageous safety feature.

Rudy is gone.

The people here are notably less concerned than us about bacteria and germs and hand-washing, but in a weird way of course. At dinner, bread is placed on the table next to the plate, never actually on the plate itself or on the napkin, and baguettes are often wrapped in a pinch of paper or just nothing at all when purchased and are carried about all over, in hands or under arms, unprotected- and yet the other day when host little-bro Francois turned his empty plate upside down on the table while waiting to be served he was forced to go get a new one because that one was now unclean. ??? Maybe bread here has some sort of anti-bacterial property, or maybe the tables are prone to carrying disease. I can just see French field medics in the Middle Ages sprinkling crumbs all over wounded soldiers to prevent infection, and then warning them to stay out of furniture stores.

Had another weekend bus tour to some neighboring villages, including the very old and historic hilltop church that was the initial gathering point for crusaders heading east ("So this is where the shit hit the fan..."). We also saw the town used in the filming of the movie *'Chocolate'* [Famous persons I've now walked in the footsteps of: Julius Caesar, Johnny Depp]. Our guide was a history professor from the school (I don't have any classes with him). He made endless bad jokes, insensitive remarks, and was generally inappropriate, sexist and offensive throughout the entire trip. I'm thinking of auditing one of his classes.

There was an international dinner at the school a few weeks ago. They had us make a desert from our homelands. I made two, to represent our culture of excess. The first was the Traditional American random ingredients I found at the store à la raspberries cake, which in the end my co-baker and I dubbed an "Amero-Hungarian Hazelnut Raspberry Tart," and the second was a huge smearing of slightly overdone Rice Crispies treats.

The dinner was a fun time. When the table I was at finally dispersed, the tablecloth (a large sheet of butcher paper) was covered with maps, diagrams, equations, and all our names written in twenty different alphabets. The other tables were spotless. Clearly ours reigned supreme. And naturally (not to harp on this, but it still astounds me) I was the only American who could be bothered to sit at this awesome international table of glory. It's especially irksome in this case because the Reigning Supreme table had to speak English the whole night anyway to accommodate those who didn't know French. Where's the hang-up? -Zero effort! I just don't understand it.

International generalizations from other people:
Traditional Chinese clocks feature a time unit equal to *two* western hours. Clocks show only 12 marks and the hand makes one rotation a day, and the units do not line up with the Western system- from 11:00 to 1:00 is a one "hour" time unit, not 12:00 to 2:00 (which would have the beginnings line up with the cardinal positions) –meaning that everything is different by one hour, and thus Chinese New year starts at 11:PM.

Especially for girls, going outside in Hong Kong with your hair unstyled is as big a faux pas as going out naked.

Mandarin is a tonal language and a single word can have up to fifty different meanings depending on its stress.

In Mexico, the grand measure of social status is the throwing of a huge party every few years –three hundred guests, invitations are something amazing like glass cups with date and time engraved on the side, a jumbotron video screen is set up, the pool is covered with a glass dance floor and a shark is put inside for show. Poorer families will save for a lifetime to put on a single party for their child, and the social morays surrounding whether or not you go or who you invite are intensely complex, and there are websites that report on the events and people to make deciding easier.

In India, parents do not accept long hair on males. Fill the urge while you're in France if you must, but don't let anyone see you, and get it cut before you come home or we'll disown you.

Weddings last for three days. The U.S. ceremony sounds "really boring."

Paper airplanes are thrown differently! Put your palms together, fingers pointed up, with the nose of the airplane pressed vertically between your middle fingers, point down, upside facing away from you. Now rotate the plane down towards your face so that it is right side up with the stern and your fingers pointing at your sternum. Push your fingers together and your wrists out and away to launch the plane. This way gives you much butter aim, even application of force, and can be used in place of a pebble when throwing things at a lover's window late at night.

Pound notes from the Bank of Scotland are legal tender in England, but almost everyone refuses to accept them.

Scots call the islands 'Britain', the English tend to call it all 'England' [according to the Scots…].

Switzerland too says "[seventy]", like Belgium and Luxembourg, instead of "[sixty-ten]" like France. This is good since it prevents errors like charging me 12 Euros instead of 72 ("sixty-twelve"). …I really didn't want to point that out to them.

In the UK "Fanny" is slang for *female genitalia* so watch out asking sales staff where you can find fannypacks, what you're after is called a *bumbag*.

More general:
Saw spherical cucumbers at Carefour.

Bell peppers are sold by the kilo here, not by the unit like back home, so you don't have to feel compelled to find the biggest ones available. Takes a lot of the pressure off.

Instead of mobile radar speed finders for traffic that show how fast you're going as you approach them, thus guilting you into slowing down, here they have street signs that will light up with a big red reminder of the limit- and they only do so when you're actually speeding (better for electricity consumption no doubt).

The other day whilst taking a photo on the street for the sidewalks of France dog crap project, an elderly lady who was out walking her poodle asked what sort of 'sadistic activity' I was up to. The explanation starts by saying that in French classes in other countries we learn that French sidewalks are covered with poo, but she interrupted me in a funny way as I started telling her this:
   "(It's a long story Madam, you see, I'm an American-)"
   "(Ah okay, that explains it.)"
Yup! Don't have to work hard to spread the good image over here, we've already got one!

The project is advancing well. I'm at two hundred sixty-seven photos. There are occasions at night when I see a prime piece of work but it's just plain too dark, and it pains me to leave it unphotographed. And there are other times when I get a good vibe and start expectantly following around St. Bernards thinking "Paydirt!" I love me :)

The protests against the CPE continue (I found it hilarious in class the other day when we all penned 'general strike' into our planners –only in Europe!). The Dijon demonstration was pretty small, but I got some nice photos out of it (see attached). The basic problem is that the French want job security, and this new contract option allows employers to fire you for no reason (or in other words; -because you suck at your job) during the contract's two-year duration (you can't just be hired to work, you gotta have paperwork).

The French aren't comfortable with the level of uncertainly the CPE would entail. Labor flexibility is essential for healthy economies though, if you can't expand with market cycles because you can't contract with them too then you'll just stay understaffed all year and voila- the situation we have today.

One sign at the protest intrigued me; it said that stable employment is a basic human right. My first thought, based on my own cultural upbringing, was 'bollucks!', but think about it, without the Anglo-Saxon influence if you can. How should we judge such things?

It started to rain after a few hours and things lost their momentum. I wonder how many political upheavals have been mollified by bad weather. Would there even be a nation here if it had rained at the wrong times back in the 1700s? Probably, France didn't revolt in a day...

Some of the schools here have been closed for two months now because of student strikes, and no one knows how the loss of time will be dealt with when the normal end of the semester comes about. Will they just push things back? People who already have summer plans could get the very short end of a stick in a few months.

There's another general strike on for next Tuesday. I just hope they get all this figured out before I need to start using the trains to travel in two weeks time.

After a brief trip to go home, one of the Finns brought me one of the few Finnish language grammar books intended for English speakers. He was impressed by my interest in the language (a rarity, especially among speakers of English) and eager to encourage it. The book is called *'From Start to Finnish'*.

Among the first things I noticed was that the book makes reference to both French and German in explaining Finnish. I guess it makes sense to assume that anyone interested in Finnish would already have a few other more mainstream languages under their belt, but I also wonder if the inclusion of the references is a reflection of a more worldly outlook. I don't think you'd see such references that often in language books written by Americans.

Finnish has no articles, and so no genders of nouns either, and *he* and *she* are combined into a single pronoun, *hän*.

There are no prepositions, it's all done with suffixes. *Talo* is *house*. *Talon, talona, taloa, taloksi, talossa, talosta, taloon, talolla, talolta, talolle, talotta, taloineni* and *talon* mean *of a house, as a house, a house, to a house, in a house, from a house, into a house, at a house, from a house, to a house, without a house, with my house* and *with a house* – with the repetition due to case and context differences.

There are fourteen cases. Finnish is a contract writers dream language. Something that would take two pages to be watertight in English can be written half a page in Finnish.

There are many instances where the only difference between two words is the doubling of a vowel. This is usually only signified by pronouncing the vowel for an extra millisecond, the sound is the same. *Tapaan* means *to meet*. *Tapan* means *to kill*. This works with consonants too. *Tuli* means *fire*. *Tulli* means *customs office*. I don't anticipate being fluent any time soon.

I saw a chess set with a Romans vs. Egyptians motif, something I never would have thought of doing. I wonder now if there's a market for historical contention chess sets. Russia vs. Ukraine, Palestine vs. Israel, England and Ireland, political groups, professions, races, the opportunities to be really un-PC boggle the mind.

Amazing cooking discovery: if you want to peel the skin off an avocado or an onion, freeze it first, then microwave it, and then the good parts will just about fall out of the peel. Amazing!

Had a cooking class at a private high school via the ESCD. We made butter-blasted chicken and wine-boiled pears. I didn't learn much really (all the hard parts were done for us in advance), but it was a hoot to watch our master chef in action. I enjoyed being amazed by the lack of concern over raw meat (recall that the French are immune to everything because of their bread). Was also a good excuse to eat something really bad for me (everything was fried in cream sauce) and in large quantities (was careful to pair-up with a vegetarian so I would get to eat her entrée too).

In France "Where's Waldo?" is "Où est Charlie?"

Cheerio!
   -Carl

how to get your ass kicked in France.jpg

Subject: **Always prepared**
Date: **Tuesday, 6 Apr 2006, 17:58**

Fast track:

Cub scouts- Turns out I have titles to English Lordship, but only in the eyes of a dozen French ten-year-olds.
Did some quality stick tying-together
Squirrel Bank not as acorn-intensive as was hoped, pondering new oak tree.

"Aight boys let's hitch up the wagons and get a move on we gotta git this here cattle to market before Winter and it's at least three-hundred miles yet to Kansas City!" track:

Went to nearby Chalon-sur-Sâon, the home of former Juneau exchange student and current Dijon resident and *Family Guy* appreciator, Cécile, last weekend to help with a Cub Scout meeting on Saturday and a recruitment mini jamboree on Sunday (turns out Scouts was a British innovation and will be celebrating its centenary in 2007). I of course thought it was founded in America so I'm feeling a bit disillusioned having heard this news, but it's okay because at least we can still be proud for inventing democracy.

On the way to the train station I was in a hurry, but was stopped by a 'guy with a cause' with whom I had accidentally made eye contact. I interrupted him mid schpeal in hurried English saying 'I don't understand', but like a good European he knew that language too. Realizing I'd been called out, I adopted an accent and said I speak 'only a little,' paused awkwardly for effect, and then said "I love you" in Finnish, and that convinced him I wasn't worth the trouble (either because it was too much effort or because he could speak Finnish too).

The Saturday Scout meeting before the big day was attended by the regular troop members -about a dozen kids, mostly girls. We did team-building exercises. It was fun to watch how certain gender differences could be overcome during these exercises, and how others were just too deeply ingrained. Whilst playing with lashed sticks [fighter jets] the boys noticed that the girls had discovered spring blooms in the yard out back and were picking them – 'how girly' they thought. Eventually though, the boys took a great interest in the blossoms, picking and arranging bouquets themselves, -with joyful abandon! for about a minute, then it turned into hardcore competitive picking and a fight almost started.

I stayed with Cécile and family at their nifty place in the country-ish, surrounded by vineyards. It was a great experience, and not just because the house had great water pressure. Cécile's family is wonderfully laid-back and open. I felt like they actually wanted to hear what I had to say in conversation (because they did!) and that makes saying it much easier, so communication was better all around. It also helped that Cécile speaks great English and could facilitate :)

Sunday's recruitment event went well. I was a bit surprised, though, when it turned out that I hadn't understood the day before what my level of participation would be, and that the plan was that I would be providing continuity for the event by pretending to be the great-grand-nephew of the English lord who founded the group, which included speaking in a crazy English accent (had that down pat – kids couldn't tell the difference) and wearing highly fashionable scout gear [see photo] from the early 50s. That hat is an original from 1947, and the legs were specially detanned to provide credibility to the idea that I was English.

For the opening I was supposed to wander past the front courtyard while everyone was gathered outside, purely by chance, take notice, and then read a short speech that I happened to have with me about being on a worldwide tour to see if Scouting is alive and well and ask if I could join

them. It was easy enough, but nothing unpracticed ever goes as planned, so my interaction with the guy with the microphone (how convenient that he happened to have one even though no speakers were expected...) was a bit choppy; "Questions? What!? Frenchguy there isn't supposed to be any interaction here. You're deviating! Follow the script! -which, by the way, says that I'm the only one on the script! Agh!" My closing at the end of the day was better. I said they were all wonderful, that my great-granduncle would be proud of them, and handed them a bunch of candy. They totally bought it.
"Est-ce qu'il est vraiment...?"

Scouting itself consists primarily of lashing sticks together (it's like getting a Twine and Twig certification). The idea is more to learn team-building and leadership abilities than it is to be able to survive in the wilderness. Times change, so do needed skills. Now your survival is more dependant on being able to work with others than being able to catch a squirrel and eat it. Besides, there is no wilderness here. Or at least, there's a village every ten miles. You don't often hear about people getting lost in the wilds of France. The kids all had a great time, and they're learning good lessons.

The local pronunciation is "scoo'tease-mu."

It all reminded me very much of my 4H camp counselor experiences as a teenager in Juneau. Our one-week camp, run once a summer on the outskirts of town for nine to twelve year-olds, was always a highlight of the year (and oh man the food was good). Like all things of that nature I didn't realize how much it meant to me until it was over. I hope those in charge of it know what a difference it made in the lives of all those who participated.

Bank- I must be honest; Squirrel bank is loosing its fuzzy-cheeks and whiskers charm. I'll put myself on the director's schedule for this week (I have a computer password, I can do that!) and see if we can find something else for me to do at the agency, and if not I'll probably call it quits. I'm still at the front desk, untrained and unuseful. The 'it's in French' excuse can only go so far (though it still works great to justify watching a lot of TV). I've been there long enough to be able to make a vague 'international banking' reference on my résumé, and since it's something that's done to be amusing and isn't actually amusing- stopping seems like a reasonable thing to do. Plus I'd get to sleep in of Fridays again!

Minä rakastan sinua,
    -Carl

Carl looks boldly into the future.jpg

Subject: **Avast matey!**
Date: **Monday, 10 Apr 2006, 13:43**

Fast track:
I miss water & wanna go sailing. Thought you should know.
Squirrel Bank is no more.
Another bus trip.
More visitors, yay!

"*My thesis can write itself, I'll see what Carl's up to*" work avoidance for students track:

I officially decided to drastically lower Squirrel Bank's coolness factor by discontinuing the gracing of them with my presence. The entire time I was there I only once handled a client's request entirely on my own, and I think giving her the information she wanted about her son's account was actually illegal. So anyway, I'm happy with the amount of time I spent there. This is not a defeat; it's a strategic retreat. I think de Gaulle said something like that once. On Tuesday I'll bring them Rice Crispies treats to say thanks (over the five weeks or so that I spent there we've had three parties to celebrate somebody's something-or-other happening, for which cake was always provided, and I don't want to show a bad face. We might start wars and throw our weight around like a drunk sumo wrestler, but by golly we're a people who will bring bank staff a dessert item when it's appropriate!).

I'm pretty sure de Gaulle never sent Hitler a cake…

I'll miss passing the hours looking up people's account information. The richest guy at the bank is a veterinarian with 1.5 million € on deposit. By the way there are no measures to prevent unauthorized transfers between accounts. Also, the code for the back door is B-2-7-1.

The latest bus trip was a good time:
We visited a fromagerie and it smelled like fermenting curds. The comté was great, and they had a laser-guided vibro-knife on a rotating marble wheel that cut perfect wedges off of 80lb cheese rounds. Glorious.

Next on the expedition was a sharp-edged tool factory that ran from maybe the late 1600s until WWI. It was entirely waterwheel driven, so algae abounded, and it still works! Inside there was a central wheel about fifteen feet in diameter that spun four smaller wheels on the same huge axle. Each of the smaller wheels had large teeth, like gears, that would strike the butt-end of a lever mounted perpendicularly to the axle. When the butts were struck, they were forced downwards -raising up the other end, which was a several hundred lb hammer. It ran at about 150 beats per minute and was deafening. And with ten indoor fires being fed off of a centralized bellows system it was probably ninety degrees inside there all the time. I imagine a bunch of sweaty deaf guys, playfully throwing severed digits at each other to lighten the mood.

Next was a semi-ancient citadel on the top of a cliff/mountain that once protected the Burgundy region from France and Germany back when it was its own kingdom. The place is an odd mélange, featuring a WWII French resistance museum, a zoo, aquarium, insectarium, and Japanese macaques living in the moat. It is, with every fiber of its being, a tourist attraction.

Our bus carefully maneuvered around the streets at the base of the towering cliff, eventually coming to a halt and idling for a moment in a big empty lot. For a moment we garnered false hope from the still-idling engine, but it suddenly shut off, and our guide stood up to gather her things and get going. Smiling broadly, she pointed to a set of stairs at the base of the cliff. The incredulous looks she received in return were priceless.

    After leaving the bus and trudging uphill towards the gate for a good fifteen minutes, the last modern structure we passed before entering the citadel's outer courtyard was: a bus-capable parking lot. My goodness you've never heard such whining. (Though really it wouldn't have saved us much walking, we were only about half way up.)

    The staff at the top are all very fit.

International Generalizations

The museum features a depressingly well-done Holocaust memorial, guided by those little multilingual handsets that seem to be all over the place here. I honestly have to say that it was a little too anti-Nazi (yeah I know, but this is a hard one to argue so at least give me credit for having the conviction to try). Facts are the basis of history, and must always be presented without bias, regardless of current understanding. The human aspect of history (the feeling that is invoked by the exhibit), which is equally critical to interpretation and understanding (and prevention), should come as a natural result of viewing well-presented facts, and not -this is the key- because the recording of the chanting German crowd is accompanied by the Darth Vader theme song. All drama can do is polarize, and that's not productive. We should feel the horror on our own and not because we're told to feel it. If we have to be told, there's been a failure somewhere. Drama does not en-gender proper empathy.

The sunset on the ride home was beautiful.

The two Finnish guys made a neat traditional dinner the other night. Pea soup, rye bread, chips, chocolate, and a big-ole bottle of [Finnish] vodka. There was much singing of inappropriate drinking songs, and in general it was a great time until the neighbor upstairs started thumping on the ceiling. I also broke a lamp (of course it's the sober guy who's going around breaking furniture).

Friend Amy from home and a friend of hers (both studying in Spain) came to visit for a few hours during their Paris trip, so I terrorized them with a plate of my cooking and then we walked around town in the rain. They were very supportive of my dog-crap project, and didn't mind looking at ten big churches in a row (all I could think of for a tour) so a good time was had by all.

News Flash of the Day: The government just caved on that employment contract that's been causing such a fuss. No one is satisfied though since there's a lack of clarity still and everyone is trying to save face (the derided PM and future presidential hopeful who passed it in the first place, the president who supports him who's going to pass the law anyway but order the parliament to make changes to it, and the student leaders behind the strikes who now have to go back to class). It looks like France's economy is going to stay on the carpet for a few more years, I guess, but at least I get to travel without any train interruptions next weekend. This of course is more important than the future of a nation.

Cooking class again tomorrow. If I never write again, assume I had a heart attack because of the butter sauce and died happy.

Cheerio!
    -C

Subject: **La bella vita**
Date: **Friday, 14 Apr 2006, 15:47**

Fast track:

Got a haircut.
Heading south Sunday night.

You know I always thought that the DeLorean should have had to drive 88 miles per hour <u>stern first</u> to go *back* in time track:

Language lesson:
"Croupion" {<u>k</u>roo-pee-yon} (*m.*) is defined as *'derrière d'une poule'* which is French for 'hen butt'.
        You may now visit any francophone country with confidence.

Moochas-smoochas:
In France, a 'French kiss' is a 'Russian kiss' because apparently upper-class Russian gentlemen will greet ladies with a 'full-on embrace,' especially diplomats, which can cause a stir. [Tragically this was not learned through personal experience].

Citadel well:
I forgot to mention that one of the main reasons last weekend's cliff-top citadel / zoo / coffee shop was virtually impregnable was that, despite being at the top of a miniature mountain, it has within its walls its own well. A pebble, watch, and shadowy high school physics put the depth of the well at over 220 meters. 6.7 seconds was the average fall time.

Found a Euro centime in the street:
-at the current exchange rate that's either a day and a morning of good luck or just good luck of 20% higher quality, I'm not clear on how the system works.

There seems to be very little coinage on the ground here. I guess I'm never around shopping center parking lots, and also coins have a much higher importance here than in the U.S., since a higher percentage of them are definitely worth keeping (1 and 2 Euro coins are in high use). Interesting mentality difference. One year in high school I made over $50 by picking up the small change that was thrown on the floor during lunch.

Anonymity:
They use a standardized exam form here. The student's name is written on the top right corner and this is folded over and sealed shut like an envelope for grading (this is the "égalité" (equality) part of the French motto, *in action*). Student evaluations of professors, however, require you to put your name on top, first thing! (unthinkable in the U.S.)

Local students also seemed to overrate bad profs. There's a bit of a disconnect between the pupils and school at this point (everyone who has made it this far is practically assured of a good job for life), so perhaps they just don't care.

Internship concluded:
Finally over! I brought them home-scorched Rice Crispies treats at the end of the day, said my thank-yous, shook hands, and raided the supply closet one last time. If anyone needs pens- call me.

Haircut!
The barber was a delight. He was efficient, artistic, and truly dedicated to my head. The quality of conversation was great too. I fulfilled my duty as an Alaskan by informing him that Texas is less than half the size of my state and he was much amused.

The most striking difference in cutting method was the use of an old-west style razor to do the layering. Scissors only appeared for the cutting of the bangs, which are now big and poofy, with a part down the middle, opening up onto my now huge forehead like a downward-facing semicircle made out of two pygmy bananas. When I woke up this morning the terminus of the part had tried to migrate back towards its normal position on the side of my head, and as such one banana had become significantly larger than the other. Had to wrangle it back into position with a comb and some stern talking.

The whole experience took almost an hour, and he must have trimmed the back of my neck at least a dozen times with three different tools to get it perfect. As a person who clearly has no clue about the proper way to manage such things, I'm used to a much more mechanical haircut experience at my typical shearing shop, the kind where the customer comes in wearing a pair of overalls, plops down into the chair, and says "Alrighty let's git this show on the road, I got a field to plow."

Spring Break's a-commin'!

Cheerio,

             -Carl :)

Subject: **Italy's a nice town too**
Date: **Wednesday, 26 Apr 2006, 13:50**

Fast track:

Saw Florence, Venice, and Genoa.
Made it home alive despite best efforts of Italian traffic.
Italian food is amazing -the Ninja Turtles would have been pleased.

"Off the star'brd bow Cap'n, thar she blows!! My god - look'it the size a'er! There must be enough ambergris in that monster to make a thousand Frenchmen smell like eau de toilet for a decade!!" **insensitive social stereotypes and swashbuckling track:**

Went to Italy for 'Spring Break' for a week with Whitman friend Wendy who is currently studying in York, England. While in Florence we met up with friends Christa and Tyler from Juneau and Whitman respectively. It was nice to see familiar faces.

Got to experience my first night train. We were bunked six people to a room high-rise sardine style. It reminded me vaguely of Freshman year, but with slightly less hooting.
    On the Italian night trains they take your ticket and some proof of identity when you go to bed and keep it for the night so they can wake you up the next morning when it's time to get off. Having never experienced this before, they got one of our passports before we realized that the form of ID was going to disappear. Of course nothing's going to happen to it while it's away in the conductor's organizer, but it was still unsettling the first time around. On the return trip I gave them my Costco card.

I'm pretty sure the screech used for the Wringwraiths in the '*Lord of the Rings*' movies was the sound of a Eurail train applying its breaks on a cold morning. Eeek.

Florence-
--is immensely touristy, but not in a disgusting way, just in a really crowded way. The whole place felt like southern California in terms of climate, and warm climes breed Americans with money to burn.

Buildings felt like cliffs, very tall and thick-stoned, just one often filling a whole block. Sidewalks were few and far between in the old city, and the streets were almost entirely cobble or flagstones -very little pavement.

The old city features great medieval architecture, dozens of immensely impressive stone sculptures with suspiciously fabulous derrieres, and great outdoor souvenir markets.

Among the markets there were dozens of unlicensed street vendors with small tables made of cardboard, selling mostly knock-off sunglasses, belts, and handbags. Apparently, this is highly illegal. The items were all tied down to their boards so that at the first sign of police the entire works could be folded up like a briefcase and made to disappear. The Italian government is very concerned with protecting the fashion industry, and as such the selling of pretend items can be punished by fines reaching into the thousands of Euros –for both seller and buyer, so beware.

The vendors had very segregated forms of commerce. Most of the people with the foldable tables were African immigrants. The Asian immigrants were selling figurines made out of woven palm fronds. The small sheets of glass with a painting on them were all offered by southern Italians (southern Italy is much poorer than the north), and the wire sculpture benders were predominantly from the area north of the Adriatic.

There must have been some sort of system of support (or perhaps control) in place for all these people. The Folders had all built their stands with the same sized cardboard, same packing tape, same white sheet tablecloth, and sold the same general products. The Weavers all had a six-gallon bucket full of fronds, the skeleton of a defunct umbrella from which to hang items for display, and the same seven or so weaving designs with red string highlights (swallow, crane, peacock, star, spaceship, etc.). The Painters all had the same pieces of precut glass and were painting the same pictures (city view from the river, bridge+tower+dome, tree in the foreground, two birds, and a shooting star), and the Benders were all making the same tiny wire Harley Davidson motorcycles. I couldn't help but imagine some sort of godfather figure behind each mini industry, meting out supplies for a cut of the profit. The line this person would walk between being seen as an angel or as a demon in the eyes of his patrons was probably very thin.

The larger, official markets that were run out of big mobile carts were also largely segregated by race, but only a few non-indigenous Italians operated at that level so it was less apparent. I can't help but wonder how often the difference between a bucket or cardboard - and a full-scale cart with a license, was the ability to speak English convincingly.

      The carts along one of the main streets are a great example of market forces and competition creating a ridiculous situation. I think that when the market was established the street was lined only with storefronts, but eventually someone put up a cart that wasn't affiliated with any of the stores. This occurrence probably occurred more and more frequently until the storeowners were forced to put their own carts in front of their stores to keep from being blocked off from the street. As this occurred, the store carts eventually displaced the non-store carts, but now that every store has its own cart in front of it on the street, no one can risk pulling back out because the other stores will take that space, so what remains is an entire street of shops that were all forced to artificially extend their storefronts by fifteen feet and are now stuck there.

Just as the oldest bridge in Paris is called the 'New Bridge,' one of the newest bridges in Florence is called the *Ponte Vecchio* ('old bridge'). It is a great example of the sort of power that the Medici family held over the city when

Cosimo the Great took control in the 1300s. The bridge, once the site of the city's butcher shops, lies between the Medici palace and the government buildings on the other side of the river. Disliking the meaty walk to work, Cosimo ordered that it become the site of a gold market instead, which is what it is to this day. Later going one step further, Cosimo, who was generally despised by everyone, later had a private elevated hallway built from his palace, over the bridge, and up to his office so that he could walk the distance from home to the capital entirely indoors, safe from rain and assassins.

"*Gelato*" is Italian for 'ice-cream' or English for 'Italian ice-cream.' Gelato is usually dairy-based but does not contain cream, just milk, and is cooled in a different way than ice-cream (they use forced air) that results in a higher density, and so is like sorbet with a milk base. So basically: it's ice-cream.
     Quality was variable. Avoid the places that look like chains, or that have huge tubs of the stuff available in bright colors. The best gelato is made by mom-and-pop-style establishments, in small batches, and with flavor instead of color (if you need a litmus test, check their Pistachio, if it's greener than it is gray, keep looking).

Italian pizza is very thin, with almost no crust, and sparse but superior ingredients. This trip is the first time in my life I've ever enjoyed what is essentially a cheese pizza, so that says something.

Heard a lot of English being spoken (tourists and students). I kind of prefer not being able to understand the trite lunacy going on around me, but I guess I should start getting used to it again since I'll be going home soon.

On our last night Christa and Wendy and I went out to dinner at a restaurant suggested by Tyler (who had to be elsewhere unfortunately), and I encountered my first rose seller. They try to spot guys out with girls and present them with flowers to buy for a Euro apiece in hopes that guilt or chivalry will oblige the fellow to make a purchase. Sitting there as I was near the pizzeria window with not one but *two* lovely ladies I must have made an irresistible target.

I only met one such person while in Florence, but Venice becomes full of them as soon as the sun goes down. It's almost worth buying a rose just to be able to have it prominently displayed to ward off other sellers (by duct taping it to your forehead or something).

You're doubtlessly wondering at this point if I ever did end up procuring any flowers for the ladies, and the answer is no. I felt it was more important to do my part to help deconstruct outdated social norms regarding gender roles, especially in a country as backwardly macho as Italy –and besides, they didn't get me any :)

Venice-
-is like Disneyland in terms of its unreal, theme park holiday atmosphere, but is actually real! I felt that it could have done well with a few roller coasters and some pirates wandering around though. It smelled like Disneyland too, mold and stagnant water, two things that will forever remind me of good times.

People do actually live on the islands, though not many, and no one in the rest of Italy seems to think there are any real residents. After a little wandering about (i.e. navigational error) we found them on the outskirts of the islands, as far as possible from the causeway that connects to the mainland.

When you go to Venice be sure to buy your own map beforehand, the ones they provide you with on the spot are wholly inadequate for navigating the confusing maze of canals and passages. Also, the handout maps are depressing to look at. It's a tangled mess compressed into two square feet and is covered with tiny black dots marking all the places where tourists have fallen -finally succumbing to starvation after days of wandering lost (or maybe those were ferry landings.... Either way-). [That might have been a Dave Barry joke again, I can't remember for sure...]

The two major symbols of Venice that are most easily purchased and packed home are glass and masks. The masks were fabulous, but available in such quantities that they lost their charm, and I decided to attempt to make my own at a later date instead.

The Murano glass, from the nearby island of the same name, was really cool. Originally settled by Romans and then taken over by locals, the Island has been devoted to glassmaking since 1291, when the glass-goblet-hoisting, glass-bead-sporting, glass-art-appreciating, glass-spear-wielding, glass-boxer-shorts-wearing (seriously, they *loved* glass) barbarian ancestors of the modern residents resettled the island after launching an invasion from the mainland -at night, of course, due to the susceptibility of their longships to rock throwing.

When we got off the runabout/ferry at the Murano dock, 'officials' (company employees that wanted us to buy their products) kindly directed us to our first glass company. The format at each place was pretty consistent. The first room was for demonstration purposes and featured the blast furnace, bandstands for tourists, two or three glass blowers at work entertaining, and the most impressively ornate tip jars you'll ever see.

People come off the boats in waves, so to avoid crowding near the intensely hot flames and breakable objects people are quickly ushered along on a tight schedule. The final stop on each tour is an adjacent gift shop packed with glass and agitated attendants, standing around looking nervously at backpacks, umbrellas, and hyperactive children.

All around the factories are endless bags of packing chips, stacks of boxes labeled "Vetro Fragile, Made in Italy," giant wheelbarrows full of more flux than you'd ever see in a

International Generalizations

lifetime of soldering, and piles of discarded glass waste that in many ways were more fun to look at than the actual products intended for sale.

Also all over the island is non-Murano glass, the majority of which is from Taiwan. Most shops will provide certificates of authenticity, or just say right on the door that they only sell local glass. If this is lacking and you really want the bragging rights, ask the shopkeep. You should get a straight answer, they didn't appear to be trying to cheat people into paying high prices for fakes, but rather in just providing really cheap items as an alternative and not discerning them from the real thing for people who don't care enough to ask. Don't let that deter you from finding a good deal though, there were lots of genuine seconds available at heavily discounted prices because of some minor flaw. Just inspect thoroughly before each purchase, and don't buy anything until you've seen all the shops you want to see -there is a lot of product repetition and there might be a better deal just down the canal.

Don't get food on Murano. The restaurants know that they're your only option and charge accordingly.

The island between Venice proper and Murano is a cemetery, which strikes me as an appalling waste of space, but probably made sense back when the city was founded. They're currently in the process of expanding it, again. Coffer dams and dredges, with barge-mounted excavators do the work. Construction there has gotta be a pain.

They don't appear to use treated wood for anything, that or the lagoon is unbelievably acidic. Pilings that looked no more than a few years old up top were rotted half way to the heartwood at water level.

    Sinking was evident, but not as universally as I would have thought. Buildings set back from the water can still be protected by raising the quays with new layers of brick. Buildings with entrances built right on the water have it worse, and many have had the bottoms of their doorways filled with brick, which only goes so far towards protecting a floor level - and that's where the abandonment is going on. The whole complex is in danger, but it has some life left -some areas more than others though.

Venetian motorboats were surprisingly un-flashy considering how macho Italian society is, though there was no shortage of fifteen-foot skiffs with 75 more HP than they really needed mounted on back. It was fun to watch the poor little craft bounce and cavitate coming out of harbors as their drivers tried to force them up on a plane at full throttle without easing into it first. Showoffs.

We tried the local delicacy 'cuttlefish ink pasta' and in so doing discovered that it would make the worst date food imaginable. Picture a normal plate of buttered spaghetti, but with a laserjet toner cartridge broken open and poured into it. It didn't taste like much, buttered noodles with a slightly seafood-ish tinge I guess, but it really did look like we were eating pasta dipped in that Armus creature that resembled a pond of crude oil from the Next Generation episode where Lt. Yar is finally written out of the series (for those of you keeping track at home that's Star Trek reference #2).

I think Wendy and I looked like fun, spunky people. Restaurants kept seating us at points of maximum visibility to passing traffic for advertising purposes. Or maybe it was just Wendy, my anti-sunburn floppy hat does a good job of abating any hip-ness that threatens to come from my direction.

Nike should abandon their dot com website in favor of an Italian domain name: www.justdo.it

The train from Venice had a bathroom toilet that was literally just a loo over a hole in the floor. Glad we don't see airplanes like that these days.

Most of the railroad ties were made of concrete instead of wood.

On the train across the peninsula we met a lady from Switzerland who was fun, adventurous, sporty, spoke five languages with ease, and thanks to the current European job market will probably never be employed again after getting laid off at fifty. She's been to multiple government-run camps to help people find employment, but the availability of work is such that what these training programs are really about is how to turn existing skills or interests into an opportunity for self-employment. She's currently working on becoming a personal trainer for Nordic Walking, which is a new fad sport that looks like cross-country skiing but with just the poles. When done properly it's a great way to lose weight and cross-train. Watch for it over there in the next few years.

Genoa-
-reminded me of the Alaska Way Viaduct area of Seattle, but with California-style houses and climate. It was the first time I had seen the Mediterranean, and I couldn't help but be struck by the fact that Africa lay just over the water, and also by a wonder about how many times locals had stood on the same seawalls from which I was gazing, looking on with terror and amazement at invading fleets. There are no forward cliffs or islands from which to protect the harbor, and large parts of the city were well within projectile range- pressed towards the water by steep elevation changes. The Carthaginians could have had a field day there.

The city was built along the shore and in the valleys between mountains that range right up to the coast. All along the mountaintops are miles of fortified ridges with walls, forts, and lookout towers. The ridges have been inhabited for centuries, ever since ancient humans recognized the inherent benefits of living up high -like defensibility and improved cell phone reception.

Like the other cities in Italy, the graffiti was intense- more so in Genoa than in any other place so far. There were also more construction cranes than I've seen anywhere else too, by a huge margin.

Motorcycles don't respect lanes at all, so at lights they all form-up in front of the cars like knights at the head of a column. When the light turns green they charge forth at breakneck speed, broadswords gleaming in the sunlight, popping wheelies on their neighing steeds. It's best to keep out of their way.

Crosswalk lights look just like traffic lights, and feature all three colors.

A preponderance of the buildings were painted to look more ornate than they really where. In some cases only sides and backs were painted so they would match the real façade on the front, but in most cases all the decoration was fake. I couldn't tell if it was cheapness or tradition.

Structurally, the buildings were very similar to those in Switzerland; large, ornate green frame stones that looked like slanted cliffs, but here with far more color above the main foundations -mostly oranges and yellows.

The beaches were garbage dumps, and the port that was once the heart of the city is now dirty and modernized, though there were some noble efforts to beautify the waterfront in certain areas (near the private yacht moorage).

Busses were used in Genoa to a greater degree than anywhere else so far; often running in pairs even, always full, and sporting cute little Italian and Genoese flags bolted to front bumper. They worked well, though the fleet was a bit old -except for the airport bus (exclusively for tourists), which was practically brand new, and a Mercedes rather than a Fiat. Clearly they wanted to give a good impression, but still weren't above gouging us – the airport line cost two Euros more than the normal busses.

Inside the busses we were all on level ground, and I seemed to be a whole head taller than almost all the locals [and remember that I'm thinking about my big Norwegian head here, so that's quite a difference…]. I would not have been popular in a movie theater.

On the way back from the airport I helped a Japanese lady find her way to the train station –in German. It was nice to finally get to partake in a conversation with someone here and feel like I was putting my fare share of effort into it.

Right outside the train station is the Genoese monument to their most beloved son; Christopher Columbus, upon which is engraved the phrase "(the patriot)". It's true, technically, but the irony was still blistering.

According to Wikipedia, at the time Columbus sailed for the West Indies -under the Spanish flag- the fact that the world is round was almost universally accepted. The real issue was how big it is. Also, the story that the Queen used her jewels to finance the voyage is fiction as well, she had actually been persuaded against the plan and it was Ferdinand who decided to go for it in the end.

Wendy's plane left almost seven hours before my train, so I had some time to kill after going to the airport. It was a very hot day and I had all my luggage with me, so naturally I decided to climb up one of the mountains.

My favorite method of exploration now is to spot something prominent in the distance and head for it, and I ended up getting about six kilometers inland, walking along the walls and paths built atop the ridges, going from tower to tower -most of which were built in the late 1700s (Napoleonic days) rather than earlier, as I would have thought. They all looked like they had been retrofitted for use during WWII, and I wondered how a soldier manning those posts would have felt from one era to the next as the conflicts changed in scope.

On the way to my first tower I made it out of the touristy

parts of the city and found where the real people lived. In their natural setting everyone is just people, and I like that.

Italian families seem to stay out much later than we're used to. The playgrounds were still full of little children at 9:00 in the evening. On my way up the mountain I found a large city park full of children and their parents. The area was home to a wonderful snack stand that had great panini and other traditional foods at good prices, as well as a wide variety of candy and sweets for kids, and for the parents a thirty-item mixed drinks menu. There were a lot of contented looking people there.

The view from up high was great -see really tiny panoramic photo.

When I finally turned around and headed for the sea I wanted to try one of the many small trails that led off the mountain instead of following the main road back. In preparation for this trip I had purchased some language books at a local book store (to learn Italian *in French*, which is actually easier than doing it in English because of the similarities) and when I babbled my semi-coherent string of verb infinitives and Françiano operators to the guy I had decided looked nice he wasn't sure if the trails connected up or not and recommended sticking to the road. Backtracking is painful, but at this point I had yet to actually make it to a train home on time, for the entire time I'd been over here, so I didn't feel to bad being unadventurous if it meant killing that trend.

There wasn't very much dog doo in Italy. Good thing I'm making my photo collage here rather than there (oops, causality fault). We're at 357 shots right now. I might stop at 365 and call it "A year in France."

Please find attached also a requested shot of my crazy haircut, taken the day of. Cheerio,
    -Carl :)

International Generalizations

Genoa pano.jpg

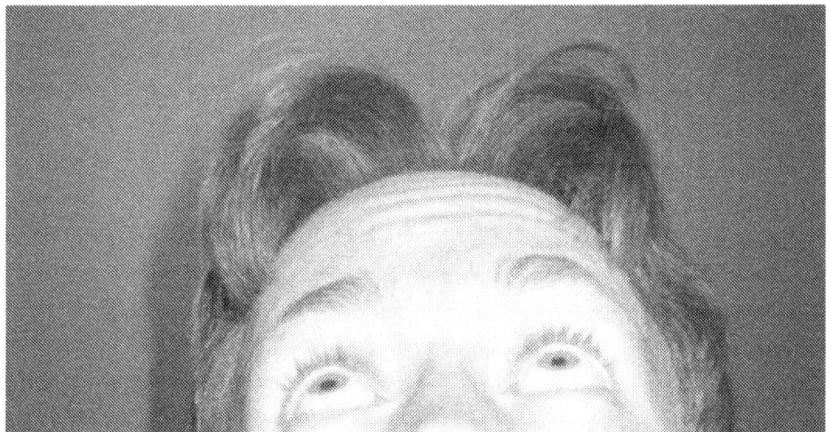
banana hair.jpg

Subject: **Hongkong drivers are crazy too, but that might only be true for when they're actually in France**
Date: **Wednesday, 3 May 2006, 21:23**

Fast track:

Went to Lyon –the little Paris that wasn't.
The French should not be allowed to cook with open flames.
Roadtrip! -looked at a giant vertical hole in the ground, then a horizontal one, both absolutely amazing as holes go.
Picked up some drugs (the boring pharmacy kind, not the 'black duffle and a 7/11' kind).

"Mommy, why does he make certain words bigger than others?" separation without putting titles on every single paragraph in hopes of making it all more manageable hope it helps track:

Lyon-
-struck me as a city that recognizes that it is not the capital of France, but does not understand why, and refuses to accept its secondary status. It seemed like they were trying to be everything that Paris is but better. They have a radio pylon that looks almost exactly like the Eiffel Tower, their Notre Dame is less elegant but on a huge hill, their 'lifejacket bins that turn out to be tiny market coffers' are *art modern* and made of shiny stainless steel, and Lyon is bisected by not one but *two* rivers! Come on people, Two! And yet Paris has won everything.

Lyon was built at the **confluence** of the Rhône and Saône, which provide a very secure location that is naturally defended on all but one small side, though oddly the old city wasn't built there, it is up farther north on either side of just the Saône, which is far less defensible spot but probably provided a more commercially efficient setting. I'm glad cash was a bigger concern than fighting.

The first river I came to on my trek was the **Rhône**, which for me carries far more importance than the other big names like Seine and Loire because of its military symbolism, as a marker if invasion progress that one always hears of in old documentaries, so I was much impressed, though there really wasn't much to see. There was very little built along the shores of the Rhône and there were few bridges. I decided this was because it's too far across, and that that hindered the forming of a small town atmosphere -as well as the building of bridges- which meant the early citizens were confined to the banks of the Saône, to the west, which looked to be about the same distance across as the Seine, and was built up in a very similar way with plenty of bridge action going on.

Lyon East features a very nice **city park** that is supposed to have a giant gold Jesus head buried somewhere in the grounds. I didn't find it.

I saw a **Subway** Sandwich place on one of the main squares and almost went in (for scientific comparison purposes, Subways involve enough preparation that there's actually room for study of quality variations[5]), but when I saw that there was a local sandwich shop right next door I was suddenly wracked with guilt and ended up just waiting for dinner back in Dijon.

Lyon had a huge **unicycler** population. I must have seen at least twenty-five while I was there, but all in the same place. I think they were a local interest club.

Lyon featured a large **rent-a-bike** network. You had to use a credit card (to ensure a return), and the bikes were very unattractive stylistically, with odd curves, thick members, and baskets ("ewww, bakets"). Somehow it struck me as a silly idea.

To the west of the city was a very impressive **Roman theater complex**. As well as being comprised of multiple amphitheaters, this site was much better preserved than the one I saw at the beginning of the year in Autun. Unfor-

---

[5] The nicest Subway in the world is located on the Oregon coast near Long Beach, north of Astoria. The food was typical, but lord it was in a nice building. It's hard to make even the most bare-bones nautical theme look dumpy.

tunately it was hard to tell what was authentic and what was not. They had gone to a lot of trouble to keep things in good repair with the crappiest-looking concrete available. At one point I was marveling at walking in the footsteps of Roman spectators, and then noticed the date 1982 drawn in the cement.

The string tells me I walked seventeen kilometers. Maybe the bikes aren't such a bad idea after all...

Roadtrip!

-to the extent that it's possible here at any rate. Thanks to things like compulsory military service (delays school) most of my friends here are old enough to rent cars. Twelve of us, representing Belgium, Finland, France, Germany, Hong Kong, Hungary, India, Mexico, and Alaska went in a convoy to see some of the natural wonders nearby (France has almost as many caves as it has federally protected varieties of cheese).

The first stop was essentially a giant, angled hole in the ground that is best described as a **cave with a glacier in it**. Apparently people recognized the preservative qualities of cold a long long time ago and would keep dead animals in there to keep them fresh, as well as using the fifteen-story drop from the top of the cave to the frozen floor for hunting convenience -"(Boop! -Falls straight into the fridge)."

The next stop was yet another cave, but this one couldn't be entered because there was a **major river coming out of it**. It was the source of the Saône (a delightful coincidence considering my Lyon trip the day before, and my Scouts-related stay at Chalon-sur-Saône a few weeks ago). It was essentially a giant underground spring in a mountain that makes it look like a full-blown river is pouring out of the side of a cliff. There are moss-covered aqueduct ruins and some very pretty green water. It was a lovely place. I'd like to come back someday and tour all the natural wonders they have to look at in this country. Generic touristing gets old after a while ("hey look, a church...") but a van and a map of caves would be a real hoot.

France says it's the country of *grottes* (caves – *Pays de Crottes*), which oh so conveniently rhymes with the word *crottes* (dog crap). See where I'm going with this?

After that we went to **Besançon** to see the Citadelle because only the Americans had been there when I went [I mentioned that my program is very separate from the others- I think another reason for this is that studying abroad has a much different feel for folks not from the U.S.; you're on your own more and are treated like much less of a tourist, and that translates into being more open because you're not being baby-sat the whole time]. When I was there the first time I missed the zoo, having spent too much time in the museum, but this time I made it, and saw some of the saddest-looking creatures ever. Fortified castles were not built for open range animals like lions.

Oddly, the most *contended*-looking animals were some **sheep** that were confined to their grassy pen on one side by a fence and on the other by a precipitous drop into the tiger pit (any sheep unfortunate to stumble over the edge and survive wouldn't have long to wait). I think I'd get a bit agitated if I had to live under that arrangement for very long.

After returning to Dijon we ordered **Dominos** and went to bed early. Dominos is better in the US, even though they did have better quality ingredients here. Back home you can get more for less, and when you're ordering Dominos it's about quantity, not quality.

At the end of the day when we were calculating who owed who what for the cars and food I marveled at what a boon the introduction of the **Euro** has been. Of course without it we'd just have done it all in Francs, but it was still neat that so many diverse people could even-up so easily, knowing exactly what it had cost them and with most not having to convert funds. Unfortunately the dollar is at its worst level since I arrived so I get a rough deal, but Alex Hongkongguy (the renter of the car) said I could wait a few days to see if it improves before making any withdrawals. That was nice of him.

Unfortunately, everyone here is on a different academic schedule, so of course that means all the cool international students will be leaving in a week, just as I'm starting to get really attached to them, and I'll be stuck here with the Americans. Eeek. At least I'll still have the French to talk to.

GO USA!

Saw a pickup truck the other day (the first in months) and it was a great reminder of home. There are few things more American than a pickup, and it made me proud of my nation's rugged and industrious foundations.

It was an Isuzu.

BBQ à la française

One of the two student groups competing to head next year's social organization panel put on a barbeque behind the school. It was fabulously French, meaning it started an hour late. A bunch of us were upstairs in the "computer lab" swearing at the machines while waiting for things to get going. Our cue to head outside was that the smell of lighter fluid finally started to dissipate and was replaced by billowing smoke plumes.

The food itself was good, but horribly **undercooked**. Instead of hotdogs they had a few varieties of thin sausages to choose from, and I picked the one that was naturally the most red/brown in color so I could more easily pretend it was actually cooked.

The meat went in a seven-inch section of baguette, with your choice of Dijon mustard, sweet mayonnaise, or Heinz ketchup –applied with a crêpe spatula. It was a **hoot**.

For games they had an outdoor bowling set and **Pétanque**. Pétanque is kind of like croquet-meets-lawn-darts. Each player has four heavy fist-size balls that are tossed towards a small target ball a few meters away. The object is, after all the balls are thrown, to have your own be the closest to the target. As mundane as it sounds there is actually quite a lot of skill involved, and strategy even. I found I tended to play by the ass-hole American strategy which was to knock the competitors' balls away from the target with my first three throws and then use the last one to get close enough to win. I try to be as accurate a cultural ambassador as possible.

Charcoal here does not come in briquettes; you get it the traditional way- chunks of carbonized wood.

I can quit any time I want!

Some combination of allergies has been giving me more of those funky **headaches** that I get than is normal, so as well as being terse and easily flustered that means I ran out of Aspirin and had to get more today. I had heard that it could be quite difficult, and might even require an examination and prescription, but to the pharmacy I went nonetheless, hopes high, ready for a fight. I needn't have worried.

France has universal health coverage and a culture conducive to medication taking, which means they're some of the **most voracious pill-poppers in the European Union**. Not only did my pharmacy have all four of the major varieties of over-the-counter painkillers, but there were none of the feared restrictions at all, they were *cheap*, came in gellcoat tablets instead of those compressed powder capsules, *and* they tasted like candy to boot. The box is nice and shiny too.

Just noticed that SNCF train tickets are printed with sparkling toner (an anti-counterfeit measure). So be sure to take that into account when you make your own....

Helvetica-*ho*!

I'm heading to **Switzerland** tomorrow to visit friends again, see some new sights, and burn a few days off my pre-paid railpass.

It will be nice to get away again too. As much as I'm enjoying my time here there are always those 'few little things' that our minds latch on to and that annoy us throughout the day, like the fact that laundry is so darned difficult (and is also time-consuming since they refuse to use the drier –such that despite putting my load into the system several days ago (I'm not allowed to do it myself) I'm wearing only four articles of clothing right now and yes I'm counting socks individually…). The break will be nice. I can go visit a buddy and not worry that I smell like a gym.

-Carl

lyonaise urban unicycle consortium.jpg

BBQ à la française.jpg

Subject: **Switzerland Redux with three weeks to go**
Date: **Tuesday, 9 May 2006, 20:27**

Fast track:

Suddenly the end is near. Friends in the other programs have begun to leave already, and next week is finals, after which Dijon is over, and I'll have ten days in Germany, then half a day in Paris, and then I'm out. -*Cheddar here I come!* Went to Switzerland again, still spiffy.

Slowly dawning track:

Banking *outer space style!*
France does not have a service mentality when it comes to commerce. That doesn't mean they're trying to make transactions harder, they just have different priorities -and that's an important distinction to remember. When it comes to banking though, I'm convinced they're trying to be evil.

Banks never want you to withdraw funds, but here the discouraging goes too far. Every bank I've been in (both of them) has had only one service window. There's a welcome desk, directory service, and lots of financial advisors with whom you can get easy appointments, but if you want cash you get to go wait in a really long line to talk to an intern who may or may not be able to speak French (suddenly I understand my value at Squirrel Bank).

At the bank where I like to torture myself ATM Transaction Fee style, they've even gone so far in the last month as to install a huge, bombproof glass airlock between the lobby and their one transaction window to discourage people from trying to get to their money. You go into the chamber one person at a time, the shatter-proof glass door closes, and the second isn't opened until the operator feels you've been properly disheartened by the limited oxygen supply and presses his button, at which time you can try to complete your transaction. How this is any better security-wise than a slit under a window I don't know, but at least they gave me the change I wanted, and, more importantly, let me back out of the big glass box.

Museum and tower
Dijon has a world-class art museum that I've been meaning to visit since I arrived here because the school gave me a free coupon. I was most struck by the statue rooms, because many of the works featuring naked males had undergone a process to make them visually appropriate for the masses during a period of harsh conservatism that took place long after their original creation –which involved the fabrication of a fig leaf carefully made to match the color and texture of the original material and which was delicately *screwed straight on* to the offending member. Oy....

After the museum I climbed up Dijon's city tower (also had a free pass) which dates back to the pre-France days. It gives you a great view of the city, but they make you go up with a guide, so I felt rushed. Inside the several-hundred foot spiral staircase (that spiraled the right direction I'm happy to say) my guide walked along the outside wall rather than the inner column, which probably tripled the distance that she had to move. She also did it all in heels.

Swisslandia
Still a nice place, still clean, and still the only kabobs worth eating (on sale for CHF 3.50! *Amazing*!).

Nick finally got a haircut (it was *long*, and this is a guy who rarely lets it go past an inch), and happened upon the interesting theory that girls rarely like guys with long hair, but girl*friends* love it, or at least miss it once it's gone.

Made nachos with sharp Tillamook sent by Nick's saintly mother. Such things can sustain a lad's spirit for months....

Saw rail ties made of not one but *two* pieces of con-crete! - with a piece of angle iron in between as a spacer. Exciting.

Made a fabulous breakfast-for-dinner at the dorm near Zurich that is the school-time home of Nick's better half Loriene. I produced two of the most coherent-looking omelets I've ever made in my life (the third was in more of an "impressionism" vein), and Nick's french toast was just plain brilliant, despite being a meal I've never really appreciated before. One of the glories of growing up is discovering that you love foods you'd always thought you hated.

In Lucerne we were sonically attacked by a big bronze thing at precisely 15:00 whilst touring the top of a bell tower (fortunately the ringing mechanisms in Europe don't also run on military time, that would have been terrible…).

Near the patch of grass at the base of the bell tower I learned the hard way that, yes, indeed, that fence is electrified. No sign on it of course, but apparently these fences are everywhere, so only tourists fall victim to the jolts, and goodness knows we're expendable. There are micro pastures everywhere in Switzerland, used periodically by micro cow herds (the herds being small, not the bovines). If there's a bit of grassland on a hill between an old monument and a river it will be used by a group of cows at some point in the year, which is a very efficient use of space that's not good for much else, and also keeps farming on a personal, human level -and helps weed out the strong from the stupid in a 'Darwin Awards' kind of way with regard to curious visitors.

McDonalds
Before he went back to Finland last weekend, my friend Kai told me that Switzerland was the most expensive country on a copy of the 2006 BigMac Price Comparison Index he had seen recently, and thus I should buy one while was there. As one who is opposed to both the spending of money when there's a better option *and* to McDonalds in general, I couldn't find a hole in his logic and agreed to it right away. See photos.

It cost 6.50 CHF -about $5.30 U.S. In the photo there is

no direct proof of this having taken place in Switzerland (like a flag in the background), but I figure the presence of a forty-inch flatscreen in a Mickeydee's should be convincing enough.

I've decided that "because a Finn told me to" will be my new pocket excuse for everything crazy I do from now on:

"...when asked why he had felt action was necessary, Brodersen reportedly told the court that a Finnish man had encouraged him to make the world-record-breaking attempt, and declined further comment. The judge set bail at $50,000 and confiscated Brodersen's cape."

Or maybe:
CIA agent: "Mr. President, apparently an unknown Finnish operative is responsible for yesterday's meringue fiasco."
Bush: "Ah see. Finnlaand got any aal?"
CIA agent: "A little bit, Sir, yes"
Bush: "-Well hawt dawgies! Saddle-up boys, y'all know the drill! Yeehaw!... -hehe, *drill*..."

Still kicking,
    -Carl

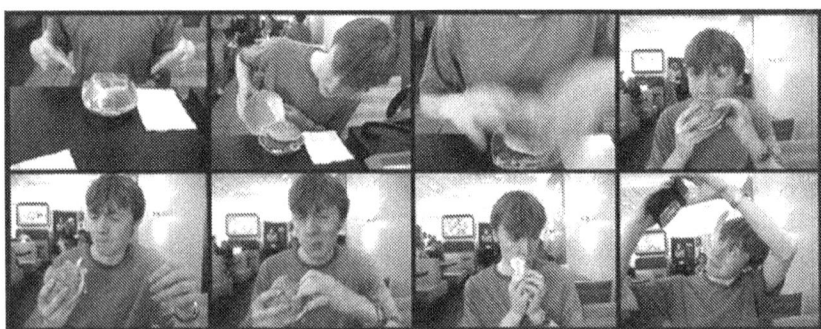
McSpensive.jpg

Subject: **Like sand through the hourglass, *this*, is *General Hospital!*-wait, no... blast...** -Last France e-mail
Date: **Saturday, 20 May 2006, 06:07**

I leave today. From this point on; I am a tourist.

I have made it an entire semester without stepping in dog doo. Of course now that I've jinxed it, watch me get nailed multiple times in the three hours that remain.

Folks have been departing all week and we've been going to the train station to give each a proper send off. It's one of those fun-but-sad types of activities. We sent the last Finn back to Scandinavia the other day, and it was great actually. After Topi had found his seat onboard the train we stayed to wave from the platform which was on the opposite side of the train in which he was seated, and in the seat in between us and him was a little girl who naturally thought the crazy people outside were waving to her, and cheerily waved back with a great big smile and much vigor. So we started waving to both of them and it was adorable, especially since the mother hadn't noticed Topi in the seat across the aisle from her and was exceedingly confused such that she had the same impression as her daughter –but she did manage a timid wave back herself.

There was a small dinner at Alex Hongkonguy's flat to celebrate my heading off the next day (today), for which he made a fabulous Sino-Japo-Koreo variety meal (with low-level spiciness for the weak-constitutioned Europeans+me). It was no fun to suddenly be on the other side of a goodbye party, but as I say toodle-oo to more and more people I'm coming to realize just how many places in the world I'm welcome now (i.e. couch to crash on), and it's a wonderful feeling that goes a long way to making goodbyes easier. I think it's a feeling too few Americans experience; I bet we'd be a much more responsible and open nation if our population had more friends in other countries. Experiences like this teach you that people are just people (yes! even outside of America!) and when you see the world with that in mind the idea of nations as politically geared entities fighting for survival is replaced with a feeling of world citizenship that sounds really hokey I know but there's something to it I'm sure. So go make friends elsewhere!

Worst film idea ever:
Titanic II

Grenouilles:
Went to dine with Cécile (of Scouts-sur-Saôn fame) and a friend of hers last night.
Transcript of events:
"(It's really nice of you guys to take me out to dinner before I go home, I can't tell you how much I appreciate it! And especially today, the weather's been great, and I love this part of town. Where'd you say we're going again?)"
    "(Oh, just a local favorite.)"
"(Well I'm sure it'll be great, and I'm starving too so I can't wait. Oh is this it?)" [points]
    "Oui"
"(Well I love it already, it even has green trim- my favorite color.)"
    "(They do have a lot of green here....)"
"(I'll say, even the chairs are green! It's got kind of an Irish feel to it almost - except for that big frog painting on the wall over there.)"
    [tense silence]
"(Oh and look, there're frogs on the napkins too!-)"
    [really tense silence]
"(-that's cute!)"
    "Oui..."
"(-and there's a candy frog on that lady's swizzle stick! And the signs on the bathrooms are frogs!)"
    "Oui..."
"(-and the floor tiles have frogs, and there's a big porcelain frog on the front desk and the pencils all have erasers shaped like frogs and the cover of the menu has a picture of a fr-oh-good-lord....)"

International Generalizations

    [convulsing in attempt to not burst out laughing]
[feebly] "(…is… this?)"
    "Ouiii!"
[…tense silence]

There are certain things in life, rights of passage if you will, that one must go through, and one does them willingly, but only after due preparation wherein you get psyched-up and mentally prepared over a long period of time. I didn't get to do that last night, and my dining compatriots did nothing to make it easier on me:

"(I guess this isn't so bad really…)"
    "(Wait, let me see that)" [looks closely at the pair of legs I'm about to ingest]
"(What?)"
    "(Hm. That frog you're eating-?)"
"(Uh-huh?)"
    "(That one right there- ?)"
"(Yeah?)"
    "(-it was a male)"
[…**_profoundly_** tense silence]

I imagined frog legs the meal as being little <u>pieces</u> meat in some sort of hunks-with-sauce configuration. But no, the frog meat is very much still on the frog bones, and it does not at all resemble the image of the guy eating them like chicken wings with a fork in the *Far Side* cartoon. There are not one but *two* frog legs per frog unit, attached via an entire **frog torso** which one uses to pick them up, making for a new and somewhat off-putting food-with-bones experience. I'm used to eating a drumstick and having a femur remain, but taking a bite of something and having a *pelvis* left over?

    It tasted fine really, kind of like a 60/40 cross between chicken and crab. Visually though, being served in pairs, the frog legs were too human-looking for me; it was like eating a leprechaun -right down to the color.

I feel as though the sauce in a recipe is often more important than the substance part of a meal over here, and I suspect that frog legs as food developed out of a bet between two chefs over whether one of them could really make a sauce good enough to make people pay to eat slimy amphibians.

The toilet seat covers in the bathrooms were decorated with frogs, –fornicating.

Possible tag-lines for worst film idea ever:
– Jack's back!
– The Resurfacing
– Alien Intervention
– James Cameron Wants Another Boat…

SNL à la francaise = 'The Daily Show' meets 'Southpark' as performed by 'Sesame Street':
The National Lampoon of France is a show put on with life-size puppets called *Guignols* (*puppets*), in the format of a news report (that is itself a spoof of one of the tackier national television channels). The episodes are scathing, occasionally graphic, and have the unqualified decency to unabashedly attack absolutely everything imaginable. Nothing is exempt, though America is, of course, is an extra special favorite.

On the show, all Americans who are not otherwise famous and recognizable are played by Sylvester Stallone puppets and all are named Bob. I kind of liked the image, to be honest, and even found myself admiring the self-assured, power-backed dude with a chin of doom and nice suit as he sat there explaining what preposterous undertaking we were forcing on the world this week, even though that's what they're making fun of –so I guess they've got us nailed. Other regular guests include Saddam Hussein, Osama bin Laden, and Michael Jackson.

The structure of Romance language verbs makes them more inclined towards humor because it's easier to rhyme. Unlike our crazy system, most of these verbs have infinitives that all end in one of three ways (specific to the language) and are all conjugated in nearly identical manners within each ending group and across the personal pronoun board. In French the three groups are "-er", "-re", and "-ir". Since syllabic similarity and rhyming are some of the core elements of basic humor, that opens up a big range of options for word play- for example this bin Laden interview about recruiting hijackers, saying they look for simple people who can't [lire] (read) [écrire] (write) [atterrir] (land)." The ends are all pronounced the same. Most of this joke comes in the delivery, but I assure you it was hilarious. Verb rhymage; it's awesome.

Random:
Busses here all use air breaks –which are often illegal in U.S. residential areas, and for good reason; they're deafening. What is more, they all have special Carl Sensors that make sure the compressors release their extra air right as the vehicle is passing me.

Hoping to avoid further food grocery shopping before departing, I'm making do with what I have in creative ways. I made a raspberry jam and Dijon mustard sandwich last weekend. Very… interesting.

There are so many national rules in this country that trivia game shows will actually use them as questions- for example: '(And now this is for win, Mr. Grangier, how long does a person have to dispute the amount of a personal check at any bank according to the federal statues?)"
The answer is seventy days. Mr. Grangier won.

Calligraphy is huge in this country, as are very fancy fountain pens. They're seen as a sign of class and financial virility, and more than anything as a joyful reminder of the bourgeois good old days.

Along similar lines, glue guns are not for providing water-resistant, fast-setting glue, they are in fact "(wax pistols)" that melt plastic-impregnated paraffin rods for use with metal stamps to seal letters and scrolls in the elegant, traditional method.

Do you remember those plastic, cylindrical, multi-colored beads they had in the early '90s? -The ones where you'd use them to make a design on a little pegboard and then apply heat with an iron to melt it all together and voila- cheap art? They still have that here! It's called *Hama*. Almost bought a bag, but the allure of 10,000 little pieces of plastic breaking open in my suitcase just wasn't strong enough.

Focus group:
Went to a brainstorming session with seven other English native speakers to help a big cosmetics/pharmaceuticals firm find a new brand name for a revamped bandage product. Half of us were American, the others were Scottish, and the difference in name suggestions between us was astounding. Guess who liked the ring of 'K-Band Pro Sport Wrap', and then who suggested 'Ankle Cozy.'
    The company had some really neat product ideas. One was a bandage wrap with ovals printed on it. When applying the bandage, stretch it until the ovals become circles- this will be the perfect amount of tightness.
    They also had bandaids with strips of silver in them for the antibacterial properties. It makes perfect sense, but boy they seemed ritzy, precious metals in your first aid gear? Honestly…. I have a box of them at home. -It was free, come on!
    Most importantly of course was that in addition to the free product samples and the gift card they very kindly gave us, they also had platters of intricate little French desserts that are like tiny works of art. Mmmm… hang on, I need to wipe the drool off the keyboard…

Okay, off to Germany!
I'm almost packed even! -though I did have to drop a ridiculous amount of money on boxes to ship items home so I'd

be able to walk great distances with just my two suit-cases (mustard weighs a lot).

Revenge is a dish best served with a baguette:
Remember that swanky club from the very beginning of the semester that refused me entrance on account of improper pants selection and I said it'd be funny to go back again and smuggle in some really un-stylish clothing selections? –see smug photo. Vive la résistance.

...
..
.
.
.
.

mixed plaids.jpg

Subject: **Eine Reise nach Deutschland**
Date: **Sunday, 28 May 2006, 15:53**

Fast track:

Left Dijon,
Survived station change in Paris,
Made it to northern Germany,
They got sausage and doughnuts here -life is good.

-10 days in Greifswald, a day in Berlin, half day in Paris on the 30th, D.C. and the North Carolinian Outer Banks on the 31st, Juneau the 7th, then Canada a week after.

Whilst in Germany I'm going to call myself Otto von Schnitzlepusskrautengescheitmeyer to blend in with the locals track:

Dijon Exodus
The last day was rushed of course, but I finished everything; cleaned my room, forced my packrat mind to leave some junk behind, brought a rose to the lady who let me use the wireless in the hotel we stayed at time and again when the school's system failed (she was stunned, I think as much by the fact that I didn't follow it up by hitting on her -this is France after all- as she was by the flower itself. Should have tried to get her number...), and gave all my extra food to buddy Alex who waved me off at the train station.
     Being rushed was nice since it meant not having time to feel melancholy until I actually sat down on the TGV. The French don't seem to be very big on sentimental celebration. At the goodbye cocktail at the school I was the only person who made a toast, and all my host family and I did was have a last dinner –I made them stir-fry and they gave me a neat little watercolor print. I find it odd that an emotional android like me would want more emotional finality than people from a Latin culture. Fortunately I still have Paris II on the way out to tie it all up and tempt the gods of doggy doo one final time.

Paris I
I was happy to see that no one had stolen the Bastille in my absence.

Had to walk a few kilometers to change train stations. Made it halfway before deciding that I'm not superman -or at least that my bags were full of kryptonite- and getting on the metro, which was utterly confusing. I asked a local if I wanted to take the #5 to get to the Gare du Nord as labeled on the map and she said yes, exactly, but then in a panic pulled me onto a train labeled #3 when she saw I wasn't going to get on it, and it turned out to be the right one. The Paris metro sucks, so I left and went to Germany.

Trains
In France the national railway service uses an upbeat *bum,dah,dah-hdump* jingle to proceed loudspeaker announcements in the stations. It's pleasantly discordant and the strange tone gets your attention well. In Berlin the method is different; the sound is the single striking of a deep bell that feels menacing and biblical: "Achtung; the Apocalypse will be arriving at track VI shortly, please remember to validate your tickets before boarding one of the four horsemen. Auf Viedersehen."

German railroad ties are the most closely spaced I've seen, are concrete, come in sets of twelve, and are housed in poured casings with lots of holding power provided by good gravel placement. It's one smooth ride, let me tell you.

Greifswald
-is the college town of Henrike (Hen-ree'kuh), another former Juneau-Douglas High School exchange student and awesome person extraordinaire. Like Cécile in Dijon, she's a Juneau person to me, so visiting is a nice step towards adjusting to going home, and she's feeding me, so life is good.

Northeastern Germany has a bit of a "Communism Slept Here" feel to it, but, really, aside from the regularity of the mass housing structures and the twenty-five foot tall bronze statue of Lenin in the main square I think it's mostly just a preconception on my part.

The landscape is covered with numerous fields of yellow flowers that are used to make canola oil. Search for 'Greifswald, Deutschland' in Google Maps and you'll see what I mean [if you do this you'll also learn if I was serious about that Lenin statue or not].

Everyone rides a bike, and 99% of the bikes' headlamps are run by little dynamos that rub againsta tire rather than being powered by batteries.

Germany has the best handicapped amenities of all the countries thus far visited. Among other things, the crosswalks feature signaling devices that make it safe even for folks who are blind *and* deaf- a square plate on the top of the button vibrates when it's safe, along with the chirping and flashing, and there is a signal to turning cars to exercise caution when there are pedestrians.

The radar-based anti-speeding signs give both negative and positive feedback- lighting up with a big smiley face if you're under the limit. So far people have been so good I don't even know what happens when a car is going too fast, but I imagine they release a swarm of robotic gorillas that capture the offending vehicle and rip it to pieces, which they then carry off to be recycled.

As well as numerous nuclear power stations, there are windmills *everywhere*. They've been derided for being ugly, but I think they're beautiful, and undeniably good for the environment. I'm sure the piles of stunned birds at the bases of the pylons are an unrelated coincidence.

German toilets are the scariest things I've ever seen. Let's just say that 'inspection' is a standard part of daily activities, and the toilet bowls are designed with a 'shelf' to accommodate this perfectly normal health-related activity.... I remain dubious, but at least there's no splash-back.

Killed the last extra day on my Eurail pass visiting two nearby towns. Everything is built out of brick, is very well organized (even in the oldest parts of towns), and the upkeep of buildings is amazing. Paint is always fresh and it's quite colorful. It reminds me of Juneau really, and even the people look more like your average Juneauite than the French (-this might just be a (mildly racist) preconception playing with my senses since I tend to imagine most Alaskans as Vikings).

Got to go to a calculus review class. The building was old and not exactly plush, and there were not enough places to sit, but at the same time there were very fancy sliding chalkboards and a digital projector on the ceiling. There's no cushiness here, just the opportunity to learn if you want to take advantage of it.

Germans take even fancier notes than the French (who already put Americans to shame) and everyone has their little pencil bag that kids in the U.S. never use, but that are everywhere in Europe.

The cafeteria food was good, though I'm still a fan of Whitman's 'give us a wheelbarrow full of money and then you can pig-out indiscriminately for the rest of the semester' system.

Germans seem to be much more concerned about English ability than others. A couple people who weren't fluent seemed embarrassed, and groups would frequently apologize for not speaking in English when I was the only person out of ten who had trouble keeping up. This overwhelming politeness kind of made me feel bad. "Wir sind in Deutschland, man sprecht Deutsch hier!" That reassured a lot of people, though probably just because I conjugated the verb wrong. Talk about stark contrast though.

An interesting variation on the English ability expectation is when non-native speakers use it as an international language (say, a Finnish guy asking a Frenchie when the ice rink is going to open) and are surprised when others can't respond in kind. If you had to learn it yourself is it more okay to expect it from others?

On the first day of grade school German children are given a large, cone-shaped container by their parents that contains school supplies and candy. Later on the images of this event become symbolic of a student's early education years and fall into the same category as naked baby pictures in terms of the quintessential 'youth photo.'

Made two pizzas with Henrike, and she added corn [okay that's weird but at least it's an established European standard] and <u>bananas</u>! [that's just Henrike being weird].
Of course, both tasted great.

Back to Berlin!
   -Carl

greifswald.jpg

Subject: **Berlin!**
Date: **Tuesday, 30 May 2006, 11:20**

Fast track:

Saw Berlin, almost kinda like it a little bit more than Paris maybe I dunno.
Leave Europe tomorrow evening.

Cloudy skies and an efficient metro system make Carl ein happy Berliner (ha ha, *jelly doughnut!*) track:

Thomas, 'professional' exchange student friend from Whitman and life-long Berliner, has been both a great city guide and guy with a floor to crash on. His local knowledge and depth of character have made seeing this city much better and more enlightening than if I had tried on my own. And he's also feeding me (I'm so easy to please).

Die Stadt
Berlin is a shining new city that openly bears the scars of its past. Much of its grandeur is only ten years old, if that, and it has been aptly described as the national construction zone. I probably don't have more than a dozen pictures from here that don't have at least one of those huge stationary construction cranes somewhere in the background. One building project near the center of town has ten at the moment -that's incredible (sorry Genoa, Berlin wins the title).

Progress
Among the construction are dozens of places where exposed water and sewage pipes have been temporarily elevated far above ground to let cars pass underneath, which means there's the occasional whiff of human-made fertilizer in the air. It smells a bit like salami oddly, or maybe salami smells like what's in those pipes. Either way I don't think I'll be going to any delis for a sandwich while I'm here.

The temporary piping and all the building gives the city the air of a body undergoing heavy surgery, with certain major organs just hanging out on the operating table while other matters are dealt with farther in.

Architecture
As well as the new glass dome on the Reichstag and the brand new glass superstructure of the new train station, most all of the post-unification buildings involve impressive use of glass in some way, with great effect. This is a dark city, at least in terms of color. It's like a lighter version of Batman's Gotham –very serious coloration. But the glass provides a great sense of transparency. There's no pretension here, you can see through everything.

The Reichstag
-is the building, the political body within is the Bundestag (which returned to the Reichstag in 1999 after an extensive reconstruction). It's my favorite capitol building. Something about the symmetry, the color of the stone, and here especially the prodigious use of glass panels all make it very impressive to behold. The security guards are multi-lingual and very polite, and the elevator to get up to the dome on the roof is one of the largest and smoothest I've ever ridden, and was itself almost worth the wait to get in. The new dome doesn't look as cool as the old cupola, but it's a wonderful idea, and infinitely more symbolic. You can walk up to the top -which is open to the sky- and look out at the city, as well as down upon the parliament below through a large aperture. This symbolizes a degree of 'for the people, by the people.' Unfortunately, some glass panes prevent the strategic hawking of loogies into the fray -otherwise it would probably be possible to meet lots of politically disgusted Germans up there, and the occasional opposition party leader.

Turns out Hitler never once set foot in the building.

The Hauptbahnhof
Berlin's new main station –which opened just days before I passed through it heading north- is a huge, shiny, multi-leveled, vaguely organic, semi-tubular glass thing, with an open interior full of lights, massive support pillars, and transparent elevators running up and down them –giving it the overall appearance of an interior shot of the Death Star.

The Wall
-is hard to conceptualize, even when you see it, even when you walk along the half mile stretch of it that's still in place. Before it was built, a concerned U.S. government studied the possibility of the barrier's erection, and concluded that it simply couldn't happen. Of course, the Soviets weren't in the habit of listening to the results of American feasibility studies.

Near the Brandenburg Gate, along a main street, is a row of bricks sunken into the pavement, showing where the division once lay. Its angular path and irregular positioning (doesn't follow the road's centerline at all) show no regard for the dimensions or curves of the street. The wall must have had a nullifying effect on its surroundings because its path refused to adhere to any existing arrangements. 'What you have built is meaningless'

Parts of it have been moved to be put on display elsewhere, and half of the largest existing section was used for a major mural project with dozens of artists invited to participate right at the turn of the millennium. The other half of this stretch was left in its original condition. The parts that have been preserved in final condition show lots of period graffiti on what was the western side. The side that faced east is frighteningly bare.

Cracks reveal that the wall (made in separate chunks, maybe two meters wide by five high) has rebar spaced only two inches apart (major overkill) the whole way across, vertically and horizontally, with at least two sets of each orientation.

The Memorial

Considering the depth of Germany's embracement of its history it's no surprise that the best memorial to the Holocaust is in Germany itself. Some nations refuse to acknowledge their past (*ahemjapan* mm! 'scuse me) while others hide behind other moral successes (USA), and some hide their personal atrocities behind more recent suffering (France). Germany doesn't do this.

It's amazing. The monument is a field of dark, gray rectangular pillars, about the size of the footprint of a grave, of varying heights, arrayed in a grid with narrow pathways in between that are gently sloped downwards toward the center of the field. When you enter you find yourself sucked into the darkness inside, suddenly and unexpectedly drowned in sensory deprivation, with sharp, angular bleakness on all sides- the way out far, far in the distance, and with many dangers at every junction.

The "dangers" (not originally intended to be literal) are local teenagers running around not watching where they're going while playing hide and seek.

Of course this playing begs the question; is it wrong to be doing that there? It's a memorial to the horrific deaths of millions, a reminder of the dangers of global narrow-mindedness and fear. Is it right for kids to play in it?

My take is that it is, but only to a certain point and in certain ways. A small child who cannot understand its meaning playing peekaboo behind the stones is a sign of hope for the future. However, raucous fifteen-year-olds screaming "scheiße!" when they get tagged is not appropriate. People cannot make light of things until they understand them. Hopefully those loud kids playing games -running past the occasional teary-eyed octogenarian- in those pillars will never know the hardship of those for whom they were built, *but they have to know that they don't know*, and be grateful for that. Once you've got that realized I figure it's okay, go ahead and play there. [-though paintball might still be considered poor form on any occasion. Boy it'd be perfect for it though.]

The Berlin Synagogue
-is over a hundred years old, and is still being restored to its pre-Kristallnacht condition. It had more security than the Reichstag. I even had to take a sip from my water bottle to be allowed to take it in, and one security door must close before the other will open, airlock style. If you're ever lost in Berlin and need directions, go to the Synagogue and you can ask one of the many police officers permanently stationed out front.

Soviet Memorials
There's a monument to the eternal glory of the heroes who fell against the fascist German dictatorship in defense of the Soviet Union (to use the edifice's own phraseology), right on Berlin's main avenue. Its golden signs are written in Cyrillic and it features a huge statue of a Red Army soldier, and actually bears a huge resemblance to the new WWII memorial in Washington D.C. - though I suppose any tall semi-circle made of rectangular stones would.

It was among the first structures built after the start of the occupation and is accompanied by several nearby cemeteries that reflect the grandeur of Soviet architecture- huge, impersonal, glory of the motherland pouring out of every crack. A monument to a grand idea as much as to the soldiers buried in them. I had no idea any of this was here, and I still can't wrap my head around it. Few recognize the role that Russia played in the allied victory though. Losses were appalling, and I can understand a certain sense of entitlement being felt. History is written by the victors.

As always, the German-installed history signs present a forthright image of the past, saying everything that must be said, giving no undue consideration to itself and passing no judgment on others. I found but a single sentence that made any sort of allusion to the virtue of the structure, saying quietly that the style of the monument reflected the opinion the Soviet Union held of itself immediately after the war.

The monument is located in the western part of the city, and after the wall went up it was cordoned off by the British and protected with barbed wire and guns.

The obligatory victory column monument
-celebrated in large part the defeat of French aggression under various Napoleons, with Prussian soldiers pictured in a large copper panorama throwing aquilae (staffs topped by the French Imperial Eagle) onto the ground, presumably to be destroyed. It all seemed ironically prescient in a 'twisted fate' sort of way -every good WWII documentary ends with people parading dipped swastika poles across a field and then chucking them along with thousands of others onto a bonfire. We're all guilty of something.

The column had pockmarks all up and down its shiny brown marble sides. They're from gunshots. There's nothing nearby to bomb, so it couldn't have been flack; it's all deliberate gunshots. Sixty years on, and the monument, especially those four copper panoramas that adorn its foundation, are riddled with bullet holes, aptly placed in prominent figures heads and rear-ends, and large parts of the panels have just plain been torn-off. Instead of replacing them though, elegantly simple covers have been fashioned and welded into place. The partial destruction is as important now as the monument's original intention.

Look closely and you'll see that almost everything of age in this city still bears the scars of bomb blasts and warfare in one way or another. Part of the reason the Reichstag looks so neat visually is that its stone facades are covered with discolored patches to repair holes caused by bombings and ordinance. Most other structures have been left unrepaired, the dings and blasts a testament to the destruction of the city. Berlin is modernizing fast, and much of its history has been restored or refurbished, but in all cases they were careful to leave at least one example in its original decayed or bombed-out condition. It's impossible to forget the past here. The whole city is a monument to memory.

Random/
Great scott my train's in like 15 minutes I gotta rap this up
Rode my first double-decker bus- which also served as a tree trimmer in many of the more branch-intensive places along the avenue. Rode past a large concert hall that locals affectionately refer to as *die schwangere Auster* "(the pregnant oyster)."

The metro is above ground, which means the city has great levels (it's not just flat) and you can actually see where you're going. It says something that a bumpkin from a city with mass transport 'amenities' like Juneau can use it with ease.

Berlin also has rent-a-bikes (like Lyon), but true to form they're way cooler than the French ones. They're full-suspension and have hot red detailing, and the baskets were more aerodynamic.

If the pronunciation of the vowel in "Straße" was short instead of long that would have meant that after the 1996 spelling reform they'd have had to change it to a new spelling "Strasse" –i.e. change almost every single street sign in four countries. Good thing.

Berlin has the second largest Turkish population of any single city –including those in Turkey. European kebabs were created here, and are called 'Döner' (which is a brand name, like Kleenex and Xerox).

The typical Berlin junk stand features DDR uniform relics, Soviet military dress hats, old gasmasks, Rubles, Matryoshka dolls, and for some reason lots of amber trinkets (that's probably the Russian influence again).

Many of the older buildings here have stone carvings of a generic Woman's Face for adornment, and they all look like the Statue of Liberty.

Saw a metermaid with a gun. I think he was a cop serving double duty, but still, I like the image.

Germany gets the Graffiti award for both quantity and quality. It's everywhere, and tends to be pretty good and rarely seems to be just for defacing purposes, though there is still a lot of tagging -which is just putting your symbol on something and has absolutely nothing to do with art.

Almost no dog poo here (only two units sighted; very tight and orderly, well-executed overall). This city gets an A+ for depriving sarcastic buggers like me of a chance to make scathing feces-based art projects.

And there we go.
Forward once more unto the Paris rode the Carl!
    -Carl

Subject: **North Carolina; now there's culture shock...**
Date: **Wednesday, June 7th, 2006 - 8:57 PM**

Fast track:

Made it back to Paris and flew to D.C. via London, where they foolishly let me back into the country.
Been touring the Outer Banks of North Carolina with my father.
It's too humid.

***Bonjour y'all!* track:**

Au'revoir France: Paris II (well, IV technically)
They were filming something at the train station when I went back through Paris so there's a good chance I'm an extra in a French movie now. I walked through the background of the area they were filming about twenty times during different scenes, so I aught to make it in.

Paris' Charles de Gaulle airport is the worst airport I've ever passed through, and I've been through pre-renovation LAX. It's too large, poorly signed, and you can't get to a waiting room with chairs until you go through security, which they will not let you do until at most an hour before your flight. I got there *five* hours before. I also had to empty my Nalgene to get my carry-on under the weight limit and then couldn't find a single water fountain on the inside to refill it (had to use a sink instead). Grrrrrrrr....

      After discovering CDG's appalling seating situation I went back out through immigration to wander outside a bit, and this time they actually stamped my passport! I kind of liked the idea of not having my movements formally marked on paper- could always claim I was elsewhere if need be, but I guess it's better to err on the side of reality.

      Whereas Heathrow gets a 7 in terms of overall quality, I'd have to give CDG a IV (using Roman numerals to reflect the fact that everything there is just a little bit harder that it should be).

Cheerio England, pip pip!

At the BA gate at CDG I found myself surrounded by people speaking English again and I felt a strong urge to adopt an accent and pretend anglais was my second tongue. I think I've gotten used to being mildly special linguistically (not all of my compatriots in Dijon could speak French effectively) and now fear being normal again.

Via plane window: England is very flat. Unlike France, it still has trees. Somehow its size and organization is just on the edge of a person's ability to conceive all at once –perfect size for a kingdom.

The Brits know how to travel. Was on a 777 again with a mini TV in the seat in front. Even though it was repeatedly made clear via crew announcements that we were not in first class (to make those who were feel better about themselves), we were given *two* very tasty meals along the way and they even offered me Worcestershire Sauce with my tomato juice. Stayed awake the whole seven hours to help with jetlag. Somehow I'm still exhausted…

Reentry into the U.S. was easy. You fill out a declaration form, show your passport to one of our snappish guardians of democracy, get your luggage off the conveyor, and on the way out hand your declaration to another guardian who looks to see if you were tagged by the first guardian for further travel-related stress. Wait times at these reentry places can be epic, but I had an easy go of it since the over-21 white male citizen line moves pretty quickly.

Let the readjustment begin!

Four score and seven-

x 2 seems to be about how many kilos we all weigh. Americans are huge and we have a tendency to waddle. Considering the amount of butter used in French cooking it's gotta be the lifestyle -car use probably. Our cars are enormous; parking spaces look like they could house, well, a house.

International Generalizations

Everything is loud. The background noise is constant everywhere you go and the volume is always turned up way too high. People talk more loudly too. I find myself covering my ears and cringing multiple times throughout each day.

American toilet paper is huge! -you could just about fit two Belgian pieces side-by-side on an American piece. I guess it's made to be proportional to our spacious rear-ends.

US TV is atrocious. Artificial drama is used to make uninteresting tripe appeal to the lowest common denominator, and the news is god-awful sludge (here I'm especially pointing a finger at Fox, and not the index finger).

US habitation sprawls. The cities stretch for miles and don't seem to have any real limits. I blame cars for making this possible.

Saw some U.S. churches while driving around. Boring! Ha ha. Nothing will ever compare.

In general, the return feeling is one of isolation. After going to a country that is so much more aware of and a part of the rest of the world, coming back to a place like the U.S. makes one feel very cut-off - as though you've seen this great thing across the sea and become part of a great society, and no one here even knows it exists.

Having successfully returned to the U.S. I immediately set about rehabituating myself to the culture by going to an all-you-can-eat Chinese buffet. I was struck by the waiter-customer dynamic. In France the patron must try hard to speak proper French to appease the servers. Here the servers try heard to speak proper English. You never hear "You want Chinese food? Speak Mandarin!" I doubt there are all-you-can-eats in France. That's not the point of food. In France it's a refined enjoyment of gastronomic art, whereas here it's a guilty pleasure.

-"D.C." not -"state"
Went to the nation's new air and space museum – appropriately, it's an enormous hangar. It's impressive to think that we went from Kitty Hawk to the Moon in just sixty-six years, or to see the Wright Flyer next to an SR-71 Blackbird.

Supposedly the Blackbird is a bit of a mess when it's on the ground. Various pieces don't fit together and it leaks liquids all over the tarmac. It's not until it's up near the stratosphere doing mach three that everything heats up and expands into its proper place. Also supposedly; there are reports of a new 'something' flying out of basses down in Arizona that can get to the border in under eight minutes - the *Canadian* border.

When cars were first becoming prevalent, some prominent thinkers in England were very concerned about the risks of it becoming possible for a criminal to commit a crime in one town and then be sixty miles away in another within hours. There was also concern about whether the human body could survive the stresses of accelerating to thirty miles-per-hour.

One of the handy information placards for a WWII interceptor said it was one of the last fighters the U.S. ever built -for that war. Someday there might be a craft in a museum somewhere labeled simply "the last fighter the U.S. ever built."

The *Enola Gay* is shiny. And it's big, so to save space the museum mounted it on pneumatic pillars to be able to fit a few planes underneath it. One of them is a Kamikaze missile jet that is little more than a flying torpedo with tiny wings and a cockpit. More than 3,000 of these were built. I couldn't decide which craft was more insidious. I guess the excuse that "it won the war" could just as easily be applied to the suicide jets had things gone the other way.

->South!
The Civil War is still playing out down here. We went to the battlefields of Bull Run and saw the attempts to be impartial and honor bravery and unity above all else: 'Here stands the statue of Confederate General Stonewall Jackson, erected just off Grant Road, where fell many brave sons from both sides, dying in the name of their homelands.' Yorktown was a lot more straightforward since those sensitive to the matter are a bit farther away; 'Here's the spot where we kicked Redcoat butt up down left and right, and over there is the huge monument to said kicking of butts, and over there is the Cornwallis Was a Ninny memorial pansy patch, and here's where you can throw darts at a portrait of George III to win carnival prizes. Screw England. Huzzah.' [slight exaggeration for literary effect].

Saw the Wisconsin, a mothballed Iowa-class battleship that last saw action in the Gulf War (the one in the early 90s, clearly it's not participating in whatever the hell we're calling this current foray). Its 16" deck cannons are touted as the largest ever set afloat and they shoot projectiles that are the mass equivalent of a Volkswagen bus with all the options and an anvil in the trunk. It's worth noting that Japan's Yamato-class had even bigger, 18.1" guns, but the destructive capability was about the same. It was darned impressive, but somehow I found it more depressing than I usually would have. I think Europe and Berlin especially made the machines of war a bit less awe-inspiring to me.

    By the end of WWII the ship, designed to carry less than 2,000 men, had over 3,000 young boys crammed inside –the extras were all gunners for the incredible number of additional antiaircraft guns that were installed just for that conflict….

Went to a European Countries-themed Busch Gardens for half a day to get my head thoroughly raddled by roller coasters and readjust to the automotive world with a round of bumper cars. It was fun, but Disneyland -the inevitable comparison being made here- has clearly had a lot more effort put into it. As well as having a personal attachment to all the movies to lend validity to the experience, it's actually fun to wait in line there because so much trouble went into the decorations. Also, Busch Gardens is even more shamelessly giftshop-oriented than other theme parks, and the German flags on the lapels of the 'Oktober Fest in June' uniforms were upside down.

The Outer Banks and its sand bars are the graveyard of the Atlantic, with more than 1,500 known wrecks just off the coast, including at least two U-Boats.

Apparently the term 'cracker' was used by Union troops to callously describe starving locals who had nothing to eat but barrels of less-than-nutritious crackers, and is taken by many the same way the word 'nigger' is taken everywhere else.

Houses are on stilts because of flooding (the water table is about a foot below ground), and most are vacation houses and condos –which drives up taxes and forces families that have been there for four hundred or more years to move. Many houses back on the mainland have the family burial plot right there next to the house.

There's a seafood chain all along the coast called Dirty Dick's. Their natural slogan: *I got crabs at Dirty Dicks.* Sounded great to me, but we went to a barbeque joint instead after my dad used his executive veto to break the 1:1 deadlock over where to go for dinner. There was no point in trying to filibuster since I was hungry too, so I relented. NC barbeque sauce is vinegar-based instead of being the usual tomato-derived concoction we're used to, so it could be considered a culturally broadening experience. I think getting crabs would have been too.

Subway Sandwich franchises are located approximately every two miles along every road in North Carolina.

Kitty Hawk

There's a great museum and park there, with a monument on a hill that looks like something the Soviets would have built. The paths of the first flights are marked on the ground and you can walk along them. There's a reason the first one would fit within the wingspan of a 747; it was tiny. It was their fourth attempt that actually made some distance; the first three were almost laughable, even by the standards of just a year later (not that I'm belittling their amazing accomplishment of course).

It was less than nine months before somebody mounted a gun on a Wright Flyer.

Orville lived to see jet engines.

There is a modern airstrip running parallel to the sandy field where they did their tests. It provides neat contrast.

It might just be me, but all the birds in the grass that now covers Kitty Hawk have a cocky demeanor. "Awww, wook at da widdu humans fwying in deir pwane!..." [Casually stretches wings with smug expression on beak].

Back North

George Washington's Mt. Vernon manor had <u>thirty</u> fireplaces running in the winter to heat it, and is sided with wood planks that were grooved and textured with sand to look like stone blocks.

    The brand of the locks on the stalls in the modern bathroom is *Hiney Hinders*.

District of Columbia license plates bear the motto "Taxation without representation" since they have no senators and that struck someone as a good place to air a grievance.

Saw two Kebab places in Washington D.C. proper. How long until they're everywhere?

Accidentally got metal spoons, forks, crab shears, a pointy can opener, and a paring knife through security at National

Airport. Either they're finally relaxing a bit or incompetent (or just understaffed). I hear rumors they're going to let blades under two inches back on again, and they're allowing knitting needles again –provided that you can show intent to knit. When I was eleven I brought an entire suitcase full of fireworks on a plane. That was cool, though only by today's standards. The line between 'badass' and 'stupid' is thin and variable.

Somehow the five-hour flight to Seattle was made a lot easier with the memory of seven hours from Heathrow still fresh in my mind. Next time I go to Europe I'll have to fly across the Pacific the week before to make that trip less of a strain.

Logic is beautiful.
                    -Carl

Subject: **The Frozen North is almost 80 degrees! [this is the last one, I swear!]**
Date: **Sunday, June 10th, 2006 - 4:45 PM**

Fast track:

Alaska!

Final track:

Alaska baby, yeah!

I am home. Juneau continues to expand in all directions. Jetlag hasn't been too awful thanks to traveling in stages, and everything here is about as lovely as I remembered – (it's nice to know I wasn't over-romanticizing whenever I felt homesick). The most striking thing is the air, it is so pure that it smells good, not plain or neutral, but *good*.

It's also warm. I came home at just the right time after a dismal Spring, but the heat worries me. The glacier is melting faster each year, and there are mountains everywhere that have giant discolored spots where the rock is a very light gray –these are areas where the snow cover has melted off and the pale rock beneath is being exposed to the burning sun for the first time in a few thousand years. I'm also worried about the conifer trees, they like a more rainforesty climate. On the upside; I'm about to go rafting in glacial runoff in a boat that is entirely inadequate for the task, and I'd put the likelihood of death by hyperthermia at a phenomenally low 50/50. There's always a silver lining :)

I think the warm weather has lead to an increase in the spider and yellowjacket population, they are everywhere now.

I made a substantial mustard investment right before leaving Dijon as part of an effort to take the best parts of my experience home with me. I mailed twenty-one kilos and it has just arrived safely, though the boxes were just about destroyed (it looked like France had hired blind, emotionally disturbed gorillas to handle the mail) so be sure to pack well when you use international post. Also, always check your credit card statement, the post office in Dijon overcharged me by almost $100, sorting that out long distance with a culture that hates to admit error won't be fun.

I've started working my way through all the foods I missed. I've had the Costco polish dog with a root bear, started a box of "cheeze"-its, and I think a three-pound block of Tillamook sharp cheddar is in the works for tomorrow. Other staples like Cheetos are on call as well.

On the plane ride up I heard a guy talking about his brother in Vermont who had just returned from Iraq. He talked about how memories come back at random, not being able to find people who understand, feeling disconnected and aware of so much more –all the things I'm feeling to a much lesser degree. There's always something out there to make your own experience seem like a walk in the park.
I think can still get away with being moody for a week or so though.

Ravens here are *immense*. Dinosaurs would be proud. I saw none in Europe.

Gas is $3.32 at the cheapest station.

Biting insects suck.

Work starts Monday.

Let's hear it for high-speed wireless and showers with the head mounted on the wall, and sleeping diagonally on a real mattress.

I'm just shy of a kilogram lighter. Yay for walking everywhere and having the metabolism of a ferret on crack.

And so it ends! Thank you all for reading, travel is much more gratifying when there are good people to share it with.

I hope I've encouraged some of you to take the plunge and travel abroad when the opportunity arises (or was I actually the only one who hadn't yet? Y'all are a worldly bunch), or I hope that I've confirmed your sneaking suspicion that you want to stay the heck home where cheddar is readily obtainable, the exchange rate is 1:1, and you'll be able to understand any charges brought against you in a court of law --and just let the irrationally curious do the exploring for you.
-Here's to the crazies!
à bientôt, tschüss, ciao, nähdään, laters,
    -Carl :)

Extreeeeme!!.jpg

-Epologue-

Subject: **I lied.**
Date: **Wednesday, 2006 02 21 - 12:51 AM MDT**

Fast track:

Canada's practically another country, I'll write about it too...

Beer and hockey track:

After about a week at home I'm gone again with the father unit to do a road trip to see the northern Rockies in Alberta. We're doing a loop from Edmonton to Calgary and back.

The Canadian Rockies and the national park they are in are gorgeous, and they charge an exorbitant entrance fee accordingly (gotta keep the road in good repair). There's nothing like bombing along a road for hours looking at some of the largest and most magnificent mountains on the entire continent, where the sense of wild just goes on and on. I had a dislike for things being so wide-open when I got back from Europe. That's gone.

The drive itself was pretty severe. I went through three battery charges and almost two gigs of hard drive space with my camera. Modern travel can be so stressful.
    Actually what *was* stressful were the obscenely low speed limits. I guess they were worried about people hitting mountain goats and elk. This occurrence probably would have been just fine with the truckers on the road, who would no longer have to weave their way through the maze of gawking tourists stopped in the middle of the highway to gaze at a generally uninterested animal that was looking for brunch somewhere in the distance. Sometimes when a goat would meander out onto the road the semis wouldn't even slow down for it, they'd just blast by, completely immune to the glory of nature chewing its cud there in the

median. I can understand though; after our seventh or so herd of nature's glory in just the first thirty miles we had grown a little indifferent too.

One of the stops on the way south was a tourist trap where they drive you out onto a glacier in giant, six-wheeled ice crawlers (spares for these things cost C$5,000 per tire). At the beginning of the road up to the ice the crawlers take their sets of fifty-three passengers across the steepest official road in North America. The driver brags that it's a nineteen-degree slope, which we thought was pretty cool, until we saw the little manufacturer's warning plaque above his head saying not to drive up more than twenty degrees or dire consequences would ensue.

The glacier right next to the one we went out on (this being western Canada, there were five separate glaciers in visible from the parking lot) is Snow Dome, which hangs off the side of a mountain. Thanks to global warming it looks more like *Snow Booger* these days, but don't let my crudeness overshadow the profound coolness of this glacier; runoff from this spot flows into the Pacific AND Arctic AND Atlantic oceans. This is freaking one-of-a-kind amazing. There is another continental drain somewhere else in the world that comes close, but the staff at Snow Dome found a way to disqualify it on "kindaaa but not reeeeally..." grounds that they didn't elaborate on, so North Americans; the record is all ours.

Canada itself seems uncorrupted by excess luxury. At least compared to the U.S. it still has a very comforting provincial feel.

['Provincial' is a from-French word originally and still primarily meaning "from the Provence region of France," located in the south-eastern part of the country. Here of course I'm using it in its corrupted English sense to mean "*small-town.*" This really bugs the hell out of people from Provence. heh heh].

International Generalizations

In line with the provincial[6] feeling, Canada and its social scene all have an air of being done on a smaller budget; in part because it's not necessary to spend money with a fire hose like we do in the US, and in part because there's no more money available because the whole population spent their extra cash on little window-mounted car flags that bear the logo of their hockey team, the *Edmonton Oilers* (two or more flags per vehicle is not uncommon). The Oilers have a chance at winning the Stanly Cup this year and everyone is really excited, especially the local flag maker.

Also adding to the pleasant provinciality[7], everyone is really nice. We passed a bus that's message flasher read "SORRY, / NOT IN SERVICE, / GO OILERS GO!"

Edmonton is home to the West Edmonton Mall, the largest mall in the world. Of course we celebrated our visit to this monument to consumerism by not buying a single thing, which I'm pretty sure makes us terrorists.
The roof leaked in several locations.

Except for that '*everyone* is nice' point, it feels very European here (most places in Europe have at least one local jerkwad, but so far I haven't been able to locate Canada's). Also like Europe; the government is semi-socialist and the accompanying tax rate is infinity-plus-one, there are a few random chateaus spread around [that's the correct English spelling, don't yell at me!], and they even use their train system still! The accent -which is rounded and vaguely Minnesotan- and the British (French) spellings are also indications of a closer European connection (as is the retention of an absent and uninvolved monarch, who I predict will be dropped when Charles is crowned, unless he decides to abdicate in favor of the much cuter William).

---

[6] like the region in France.
[7] -the Provence region, of France.

Besides the occasional sandstone government building that looks like something straight out of western Switzerland, everything is strip malls and chain stores, cast right from a mold. Canada does not have a lot of old grandness out west. The town I'm in right now is barely over fifty years old.

We went to a farmers market on day two and I was feeling chagrined by the fact that almost every single booth had at least one hottie working there to enhance sales. After looking around some though, and taking note of the guys too, it occurred to me that these weren't hired guns at all, Canada is just plain attractive. And better still, when you make that accidental flash of eye contact with someone, they don't just look away and pretend to be distracted, they look away for just a second, *and then glance back and smile*! Might have to move here for a few years.

The body imaged forced on women and young girls up here is the worst I've ever seen though. Parts of Europe (Italy especially) actually had pretty reasonable representations in their advertisements, but Canada is over the top and into unhealthy. The concern seems to spread beyond ads too, lots of middle-of-nowhere stores had "gas, liquor, & beauty salon" or something along those lines. I'm not sure which came first; the hotties or the advertising.

Traffic patterns in Canada suck. There are never any turn lanes, so to go left you have to block an entire lane of traffic while waiting, and then one or two cars can zip through the intersection after the light turns red. Also, the merging lanes are inadequate. In one place our merging lane merged into a second merging lane that then merged into the real lane, all this in the space of about twenty meters ("That's right American drivers, the *metric system, Bwahahahahahaha!*" –Canadian Department of Motor Vehicles).

Part of a continual effort to crack down on bad driving is the putting up of simple yet grim signs saying "fatality" to mark where people have been killed. I suspect most of these poor people were American tourists trying to turn left.

It's nice to see French again (after two whole weeks), even if it's because a small portion of the population forced in an unreciprocated law that everything must be in both languages instead of it being because lots of people here speak French and thus it's the logical thing to do.

Québec (which, if you drop the accent mark and pretend it's a compound word, translates to "only beak") is home of the Québécois, who are even more protective of their language than the French. The Académie Française allows many foreign (English) words into the official dictionaries of France, but people from Québec insist on using brand new, wholly French words. As embattled as they feel (what with the Canadian English speakers having a culture too and all) they're naturally pretty picky about the language, even though the French get the most credit for being stogy about language.

Apparently French people can't stand Quebec accents. When I started learning the language I thought they were easier to understand because of the English influence over pronunciation. Now I find High French much easier to comprehend.

The signs for the Canadian McDonalds franchises way up on their posts bear a remarkable resemblance to the victory staffs (aquilae) you see on the map on the first page of every *'Asterix and Obelix'* book, jammed into the earth to mark the conquests of the Roman Empire. Same concept I guess.

On the middle part of the giant yellow M is a tiny red maple leaf, which makes for a nice personal touch. I think it'd be neat if other countries could have this honor too. France could have a cock ["rooster"- minds out of the gutter please], Britain a crown perhaps, China a hammer and sickle, etc. Here, see if you can match the McDonalds sign to its host country:

McDonalds signs.jpg

Did I mention that '[*provincial*]'[8] when used as slang means 'backward and hokey'? (aw, really I have nothing against them, they're just easy to make fun of, which of course is a good reason to do it).

How long until automatic faucets and other washroom fixtures no longer come with stickers identifying them as automatic so people don't get confused by the lack of knobs?

How long until .com .org .net .edu .gov etc. are all eliminated because they're no-longer necessary, or just replaced by a single standardized ending, like the name of the emperor of the world when this finally happens?
www.[---------].oprah

---time passes and distance goes by---

Canada just lost the Stanley Cup. 3-1. I think I heard a scream from a distraught fan somewhere in the distance, but I'm not sure, it might have been a horse dying.

At dinner tonight the game was on the restaurant's bigscreen. Every patron who walked in would frantically run up to the front desk and ask the hostess what the score was in case something had happened between their car radio and the front door. But it's all over now, and the temperature has dropped precipitously in the last two minutes. It might be wise to postpone our flight out tomorrow and just hunker down in the hotel for the day.

In another odd twist of places-I've-been-to-recently fate, the cup winners are the North Carolina team. I wonder if anyone in NC even noticed.

---

[8] Provence, France, see map:

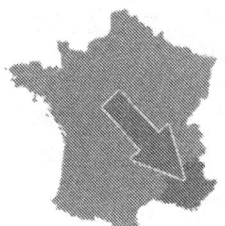

In Canada when the retention of luck is desired, they say "touch wood" and there is no knocking is involved.

Alberta has a real labor-shortage problem. Almost every place we went into had a *help wanted* sign. People in places like Dairy Queen can get C$15 an hour because it's so difficult to get people. The cause is the booming oil industry, which offers people who'd otherwise be managing a deep-fryer thirty bucks an hour to go work on a rig in the boonies. It's hard to compete with that. As a result, Alberta has lowered its minimum working age to twelve (for certain positions).

There is supposed to be more oil contained in the petroleum sand fields of Alberta than in the whole of the Middle East, it's just a question of being able to extract it (the current method uses too much water and is highly destructive).

Saw a billboard for beauty products that featured a lithe-looking bride, posted next to a law firm that specializes in divorces. Hee hee.

Humans being the fickle and unpredictable creatures that we are, I think it's unrealistic to ask brides and grooms to promise to be married forever. They should ask instead if you take this person to be your lawfully wedded husband / wife and *intend* to have and to hold them, for better or for worse, richer or poorer... etc.

"Do you intend?"
"-I do."
"And is it your current plan that…?"
"-it is."

From a museum in Calgary: supposedly the two-fingered salute insult in England stems from the Hundred Years War, when the French, in a typical display of not really dealing with the problem directly, responded to the increasing threat posed by British archers on the battlefield not by training their own bowmen, but by threatening to cut off the arrow-shooting fingers of any archer that was captured. The 'salute' was a defiant flaunting of said deadly fingers.

The idea that medieval knights were most often killed by exhaustion rather than by the enemy, and that they had to be lifted onto their horses with cranes, all because their armor was so heavy, is a total myth. A full suit weighed around thirty to forty kilos. A full kit for a WWI soldier was between sixty and a hundred (though, granted, didn't take the form of a personal dutch oven).

The name of the Klingon Homeworld is Qu'noS, but they always refer to it as 'The Homeworld' because not enough people know that. (That's reference #3. Woot!)

Well folks, they've just closed the door to the plane (Bombardier Q-200 turbojet), and the flight attendant is working her way down the aisle telling aviation misfits like me to turn it off. The Air Force mechanic seated next to me says they're not really worried about headphones and laptops in and of themselves, they're actually concerned that you have a signal jammer *hidden inside* an electronic device, so you have to put them away for take-off and landing (when pilots rely on jammable equipment the most). It's silly of course, since the obvious workaround for this is to just put your jammer in a non-electronic device like a teddy bear or a large wheel of cheese. Silly. In the end, whether I decide to abide by this rule or not makes absolutely no difference for this flight for two big reasons:

1) apparently all passenger planes fly with an unjamable gyroscope system as a backup that was the primary method of navigation for decades before radar became standard, and

2) my battery is about to die.

It's nice when things are so simple.

Be well!
    -Carl :)

Carl Brodersen wrote 'International Generalizations' as a college junior and foreign exchange student living in Dijon, France. He is fabulously handsome.

the horror.jpg

www.ingramcontent.com/pod-product-compliance
Lightning Source LLC
Chambersburg PA
CBHW020000050426
42450CB00005B/259